Bloom's
GUIDES

Ernest Hemingway's
A Farewell to Arms

The Adventures of Huckleberry Finn

All the Pretty Horses

Animal Farm

The Autobiography of Malcolm X

The Awakening

The Bell Jar

Beloved

Beowulf

Black Boy

The Bluest Eye

Brave New World

The Canterbury Tales

Catch-22

The Catcher in the Rye

The Chosen

The Crucible

Cry, the Beloved Country

Death of a Salesman

Fahrenheit 451

A Farewell to Arms

Frankenstein

The Glass Menagerie

The Grapes of Wrath

Great Expectations

The Great Gatsby

Hamlet

The Handmaid's Tale

Heart of Darkness

The House on Mango Street

I Know Why the Caged Bird Sings

The Iliad

Invisible Man

Jane Eyre

The Joy Luck Club

The Kite Runner

Lord of the Flies

Macbeth

Maggie: A Girl of the Streets

The Member of the Wedding

The Metamorphosis

Native Son

Night

1984

The Odyssey

Oedipus Rex

Of Mice and Men

One Hundred Years of Solitude

Pride and Prejudice

Ragtime

A Raisin in the Sun

The Red Badge of Courage

Romeo and Juliet

The Scarlet Letter

A Separate Peace

Slaughterhouse-Five

Snow Falling on Cedars

The Stranger

A Streetcar Named Desire

The Sun Also Rises

A Tale of Two Cities

Their Eyes Were Watching God

The Things They Carried

To Kill a Mockingbird

Uncle Tom's Cabin

The Waste Land

Wuthering Heights

Bloom's
GUIDES

Ernest Hemingway's
A Farewell to Arms

Edited & with an Introduction
by Harold Bloom

BLOOM'S
LITERARY CRITICISM
An imprint of Infobase Publishing

Bloom's Guides: A Farewell to Arms

Copyright © 2010 by Infobase Publishing

Introduction © 2010 by Harold Bloom

Bloom's Literary Criticism
An imprint of Infobase Publishing
132 West 31st Street
New York, NY 10001

800

HEMINGWAY

376-5404

Library of Congress Cataloging-in-Publication Data
Ernest Hemingway's A farewell to arms / edited and with an introduction by Harold Bloom.
    p. cm. — (Bloom's guides)
  Includes bibliographical references and index.
  ISBN 978-1-60413-572-5
  1. Hemingway, Ernest, 1899–1961. Farewell to arms. 2. World War, 1914–1918—United States—Literature and the war. I. Bloom, Harold. II. Title. III. Series.
  PS3515.E37F35355 2010
  813'.52—dc22
                              2009019581

Bloom's Literary Criticism books are available at special discounts when purchased in bulk quantities for businesses, associations, institutions, or sales promotions. Please call our Special Sales Department in New York at (212) 967–8800 or (800) 322–8755.

You can find Bloom's Literary Criticism on the World Wide Web at http://www.chelseahouse.com

Contributing Editor: Portia Weiskel
Cover design by Takeshi Takahashi
Printed in the United States of America
IBT IBT 10 9 8 7 6 5 4 3 2 1
This book is printed on acid-free paper.

Contents

Introduction

HAROLD BLOOM

I

Hemingway freely proclaimed his relationship to *Huckleberry Finn*, and there is some basis for the assertion, except that there is little in common between the rhetorical stances of Twain and Hemingway. Kipling's *Kim*, in style and mode, is far closer to *Huckleberry Finn* than anything Hemingway wrote. The true accent of Hemingway's admirable style is to be found in an even greater and more surprising precursor:

This grass is very dark to be from the white heads of old mothers,
Darker than the colorless beards of old men,
Dark to come from under the faint red roofs of mouths.

Or again:

I clutch the rails of the fence, my gore drips, thinn'd with the ooze of my skin,
I fall on the weeds and stones,
The riders spur their unwilling horses, haul close,
Taunt my dizzy ears and beat me violently over the head with whip-stocks.
Agonies are one of my changes of garments,
I do not ask the wounded person how he feels, I myself become the wounded person,
My hurts turn livid upon me as I lean on a cane and observe.

Hemingway is scarcely unique in not acknowledging the paternity of Walt Whitman; T.S. Eliot and Wallace Stevens are far closer to Whitman than William Carlos Williams and Hart Crane were, but literary influence is a paradoxical and antithetical process, about which we continue to know all too little. The profound affinities between Hemingway, Eliot, and Stevens are not accidental but are family resemblances due to the repressed but crucial relation each had to Whitman's work. Hemingway characteristically boasted (in a letter to Sara Murphy, February 72, 1936) that he had knocked Stevens down quite handily: " . . . for statistics sake Mr. Stevens is 6 feet 2 weighs 522 lbs. and . . . when he hits the ground it is highly spectaculous." Since this match between the two writers took place in Key West on February 19, 1936, I am moved, as a loyal Stevensian, for statistics' sake to point out that the victorious Hemingway was born in 1899, and the defeated Stevens in 1879, so that the novelist was then going on thirty-seven, and the poet verging on fifty-seven. The two men doubtless despised each other, but in the letter celebrating his victory Hemingway calls Stevens "a damned fine poet," and Stevens always affirmed that Hemingway was essentially a poet, a judgment concurred in by Robert Penn Warren when he wrote that Hemingway "is essentially a lyric rather than a dramatic writer." Warren compared Hemingway to Wordsworth, which is feasible, but the resemblance to Whitman is far closer. Wordsworth would not have written, "I am the man, I suffer'd, I was there," but Hemingway almost persuades us he would have achieved that line had not Whitman set it down first.

II

It is now almost a half century since Hemingway's suicide, and some aspects of his permanent canonical status seem beyond doubt. Only a few modern American novels seem certain to endure: *The Sun Also Rises*, *The Great Gatsby*, *Miss Lonelyhearts*, *The Crying of Lot 49*, and at least several by Faulkner, including *As I Lay Dying*, *Sanctuary*, *Light in August*, *The Sound and the Fury*, and *Absalom, Absalom!* Two dozen stories by Hemingway could be added to the group, indeed perhaps all of *The First Forty-Nine Stories*. Faulkner is an eminence apart, but critics agree that Hemingway and Fitzgerald are his nearest rivals, largely on the strength of their shorter fiction. What seems unique is that Hemingway is the only American writer of prose fiction in this century who, as a stylist, rivals the principal poets: Stevens, Eliot, Frost, Hart Crane, aspects of Pound, W.C. Williams, Robert Penn Warren, and Elizabeth Bishop. This is hardly to say that Hemingway, at his best, fails at narrative or the representation of character. Rather, his peculiar excellence is closer to Whitman than to Twain, closer to Stevens than to Faulkner, and even closer to Eliot than to Fitzgerald, who was his friend and rival. He is an elegiac poet who mourns the self, who celebrates the self (rather less effectively) and who suffers divisions in the self. In the broadest tradition of American literature, he stems ultimately from the Emersonian reliance on the god within, which is the line of Whitman, Thoreau, and Dickinson. He arrives late and dark in this tradition and is one of its negative theologians, as it were, but as in Stevens the negations, the cancellings are never final. Even the most ferocious of his stories, say "God Rest You Merry, Gentlemen" or "A Natural History of the Dead," can be said to celebrate what we might call the Real Absence. Doc Fischer, in "God Rest You Merry, Gentlemen," is a precursor of Nathanael West's Shrike in *Miss Lonelyhearts*, and his savage, implicit religiosity prophesies not only Shrike's Satanic stance but the entire demonic world of Pynchon's explicitly paranoid or Luddite visions. Perhaps there was a nostalgia for a Catholic order always abiding in Hemingway's consciousness, but the cosmos of his fiction, early and late, is American Gnostic, as it was in Melville, who first developed so strongly the negative side of the Emersonian religion of self-reliance.

III

Hemingway notoriously and splendidly was given to overtly agonistic images whenever he described his relationship to canonical writers, including Melville, a habit of description in which he has been followed by his true ephebe, Norman Mailer. In a grand letter (September 6–7, 1949) to his publisher, Charles Scribner, he charmingly confessed, "Am a man without any ambition, except to be champion of the world, I wouldn't fight Dr. Tolstoi in a 20 round bout because I know he would knock my ears off." This modesty passed quickly, to be followed by, "If I can live to 60 I can beat him. (MAYBE)." Since the rest of the letter counts Turgenev, de Maupassant, Henry James, even Cervantes, as well as Melville and Dostoyevski, among the defeated, we can join Hemingway, himself, in admiring his extraordinary self-confidence. How justified was it, in terms of his ambitions?

It could be argued persuasively that Hemingway is the best short-story writer in the English language from Joyce's *Dubliners* until the present. The aesthetic dignity of the short story need not be questioned, and yet we seem to ask more of a canonical writer. Hemingway wrote *The Sun Also Rises* and not *Ulysses*, which is only to say that his true genius was for very short stories and hardly at all for extended narrative. Had he been primarily a poet, his lyrical gifts would have sufficed: we do not hold it against Yeats that his poems, not his plays, are his principal glory. Alas, neither Turgenev nor Henry James, neither Melville nor Mark Twain provide true agonists for Hemingway. Instead, de Maupassant is the apter rival. Of Hemingway's intensity of style in the briefer compass, there is no question, but even *The Sun Also Rises* reads now as a series of epiphanies, of brilliant and memorable vignettes.

Much that has been harshly criticized in Hemingway, particularly in *For Whom the Bell Tolls*, results from his difficulty in adjusting his gifts to the demands of the novel. Robert Penn Warren suggests that Hemingway is successful when his "system of ironies and understatements is coherent." When incoherent, then, Hemingway's rhetoric fails as persuasion, which is to say, we read *To Have and Have Not* or *For Whom the Bell Tolls*, and we are all too aware that the system of tropes is primarily what we are offered. Warren believes this not to be true of *A Farewell to Arms*, yet even the celebrated close of the novel seems now a worn understatement:

> But after I had got them out and shut the door and turned off the light it wasn't any good. It was like saying good-by to a statue. After a while I went out and left the hospital and walked back to the hotel in the rain.

Contrast this to the close of "Old Man at the Bridge," a story only two and a half pages long:

There was nothing to do about him. It was Easter Sunday and the Fascists were advancing toward the Ebro. It was a gray overcast day with a low ceiling so their planes were not up. That and the fact that cats know how to look after themselves was all the good luck that old man would ever have.

The understatement continues to persuade here because the stoicism remains coherent, and is admirably fitted by the rhetoric. A very short story concludes itself by permanently troping the mood of a particular moment in history. Vignette is Hemingway's natural mode, or call it hardedged vignette: a literary sketch that somehow seems to be the beginning or end of something longer, yet truly is complete in itself. Hemingway's style encloses what ought to be unenclosed, so that the genre remains subtle yet trades its charm for punch. But a novel of 340 pages (*A Farewell to Arms*) which I have just finished reading again (after twenty years away from it) cannot sustain itself on the rhetoric of vignette. After many understatements, too many, the reader begins to believe that he is reading a Hemingway imitator, like the accomplished John O'Hara, rather than the master himself. Hemingway's notorious fault is the monotony of repetition, which becomes a dulling litany in a somewhat less accomplished imitator like Nelson Algren, and sometimes seems self-parody when we must confront it in Hemingway.

Nothing is got for nothing, and a great style generates defenses in us, particularly when it sets the style of an age, as the Byronic Hemingway did. As with Byron, the color and variety of the artist's life becomes something of a veil between the work and our aesthetic apprehension of it. Hemingway's career included four marriages (and three divorces); service as an ambulance driver for the Italians in World War I (with an honorable wound); activity as a war correspondent in the Greek-Turkish War (1922), the Spanish Civil War (1937–39), the Chinese-Japanese War (1941) and the war against Hitler in Europe (1944–45). Add big-game hunting and fishing, safaris, expatriation in France and Cuba, bullfighting, the Nobel

Prize, and ultimate suicide in Idaho, and you have an absurdly implausible life, apparently lived in imitation of Hemingway's own fiction. The final effect of the work and the life together is not less than mythological, as it was with Byron and with Whitman and with Oscar Wilde. Hemingway now is myth, and so is permanent as an image of American heroism or perhaps more ruefully the American illusion of heroism. The best of Hemingway's work, the stories and *The Sun Also Rises*, are also a permanent part of the American mythology. Faulkner, Stevens, Frost, perhaps Eliot, and Hart Crane were stronger writers than Hemingway, but he alone in this American century has achieved the enduring status of myth.

IV

If *A Farewell to Arms* fails to sustain itself as a unified novel, it does remain Hemingway's strongest work after the frequent best of the short stories and *The Sun Also Rises*. It also participates in the aura of Hemingway's mode of myth, embodying as it does not only Hemingway's own romance with Europe but the permanent vestiges of our national romance with the Old World. The death of Catherine represents not the end of that affair but its perpetual recurrence. I assign classic status in the interpretation of that death to Leslie Fiedler, with his precise knowledge of the limits of literary myth: "Only the dead woman becomes neither a bore nor a mother; and before Catherine can quite become either she must die, killed not by Hemingway, of course, but by childbirth!" Fiedler finds a touch of Poe in this, but Hemingway seems to me far healthier. Death, to Poe, is after all less a metaphor for sexual fulfillment than it is an improvement over mere coition, since Poe longs for a union in essence and not just in act.

Any feminist critic who resents that too lovely Hemingwayesque ending, in which Frederic Henry gets to walk away in the rain while poor Catherine takes the death for both of them, has my sympathy, if only because this sentimentality that mars the aesthetic effect is certainly the mask for a male resentment and fear of women. Hemingway's symbolic rain is read by Louis L. Martz as the inevitable trope for pity, and by

Malcolm Cowley as a conscious symbol for disaster. A darker interpretation might associate it with Whitman's very American confounding of night, death, the mother, and the sea, a fourfold mingling that Whitman bequeathed to Wallace Stevens, T.S. Eliot, and Hart Crane, among many others. The death of the beloved woman in Hemingway is part of that tropological cosmos, in which the moist element dominates because death the mother is the true image of desire. For Hemingway, the rain replaces the sea and is as much the image of longing as the sea is in Whitman or Hart Crane.

Robert Penn Warren, defending a higher estimate of *A Farewell to Arms* than I can achieve, interprets the death of Catherine as the discovery that "the attempt to find a substitute for universal meaning in the limited meaning of the personal relationship is doomed to failure." Such a reading, though distinguished, seems to me to belong more to the literary cosmos of T.S. Eliot than to that of Hemingway. Whatever nostalgia for transcendental verities Hemingway may have possessed, his best fiction invests its energies in the representation of personal relationships and hardly with the tendentious design of exposing their inevitable inadequacies. If your personal religion quests for the matador as messiah, then you are likely to seek in personal relationships something of the same values enshrined in the ritual of bull and bullfighter: courage, dignity, the aesthetic exaltation of the moment, and an all but suicidal intensity of being—the sense of life gathered to a crowded perception and graciously open to the suddenness of extinction. That is a vivid but an unlikely scenario for an erotic association, at least for any that might endure beyond a few weeks.

Wyndham Lewis categorized Hemingway by citing Walter Pater on Prosper Merimée: "There is the formula ... the enthusiastic amateur of rude, crude, naked force in men and women. ... Painfully distinct in outline, inevitable to sight, unrelieved, there they stand." Around them, Pater added, what Merimée gave you was "neither more nor less than empty space." I believe that Pater would have found more than that in Hemingway's formula, more in the men and women, and something other than empty space in their ambiance. Perhaps by way of Joseph Conrad's influence on him, Hemingway had absorbed part at least of what is most meaningful in Pater's aesthetic impressionism. Hemingway's women and men know, with Pater, that we have an interval, and then our place knows us no more. Our one chance is to pack that interval with the multiplied fruit of consciousness, with the solipsistic truths of perception and sensation. What survives time's ravages in *A Farewell to Arms* is precisely Hemingway's textually embodied knowledge that art alone apprehends the moments of perception and sensation and so bestows upon them their privileged status. Consider the opening paragraph of chapter 16:

That night a bat flew into the room through the open door that led onto the balcony and through which we watched the night over the roofs of the town. It was dark in our room except for the small light of the night over the town and the bat was not frightened but hunted in the room as though he had been outside. We lay and watched him and I do not think he saw us because we lay so still. After he went out we saw a searchlight come on and watched the beam move across the sky and then go off and it was dark again. A breeze came in the night and we heard the men of the anti-aircraft gun on the next roof talking. It was cool and they were putting on their capes. I worried in the night about some one coming up but Catherine said they were all asleep. Once in the night we went to sleep and when I woke she was not there but I heard her coming along the hall and the door opened and she came back to the bed and said it was all right she had been downstairs and they were all asleep. She had been outside Miss Van Campen's door and heard her breathing in her sleep. She brought crackers and we ate them and drank some vermouth. We were very hungry but she said that would all have to be gotten out of me in the morning. I went to sleep again in the morning when it was light and when I was awake I found she was gone again. She came in looking fresh and lovely and sat on the bed and the sun rose while I had the thermometer in my mouth and we smelled the dew on the roofs and then the coffee of the men at the gun on the next roof.

The flight of the bat, the movement of the searchlight's beam and of the breeze, the overtones of the antiaircraft gunners blend into the light of the morning to form a composite epiphany of what it is that Frederic Henry has lost when he finally walks back to the hotel in the rain. Can we define that loss? As befits the aesthetic impressionism of Pater, Conrad, Stephen Crane, and Hemingway, it is in the first place a loss of vividness and intensity in the world as experienced by the senses. In the aura of his love for Catherine, Frederic Henry knows the fullness of "It was dark," and "It was cool," and the smell of the dew on the roofs, and the aroma of the coffee being enjoyed by the antiaircraft gunners. We are reminded that Pater's crucial literary ancestors were the unacknowledged Ruskin and the hedonistic visionary Keats, the Keats of the "Ode on Melancholy." Hemingway, too, particularly in *A Farewell to Arms*, is an heir of Keats, with the poet's passion for sensuous immediacy, in all of its ultimate implications. Is not Catherine Barkley a belated and beautiful version of the goddess Melancholy, incarnating Keats's "Beauty that must die"? Hemingway, too, exalts that quester after the Melancholy,

> whose strenuous tongue
> Can burst Joy's grape against his palate fine;
> His soul shall taste the sadness of her might,
> And be among her cloudy trophies hung.

Biographical Sketch

In his introduction to *Men at War* (1942), Ernest Hemingway wrote, "A writer's job is to tell the truth." In 1948, with much of his published work behind him, he wrote that

> [truth was] made of knowledge, experience, wine, bread, oil, salt, vinegar, bed, early mornings, nights, days, the sea, men, women, dogs, beloved motor cars, bicycles, hills and valleys, the appearance and disappearance of trains on straight and curved tracks (xv).

This mostly practical and prosaic list reminds us that Hemingway was trained as a journalist to see and record objectively what is taking place in front of his eyes, but the cumulative effect of stringing together these particular words is as evocative as it is pragmatic. Hemingway was not a metaphysical thinker, nor was he religious in any formal sense, but his list of "truth things" manifests a profound reverence for the tangible details of daily life and the natural world. It is possible to trace this deepening reverence through his life and work as it would become increasingly self-defining and self-sustaining.

Hemingway was born on July 21, 1899, into relatively privileged circumstances: his family (parents, a brother, and four sisters) had talent, financial means, and educational opportunity, and they lived in the respectable and comfortable community of Oak Park, Illinois. Although Hemingway was an able and engaged student and spent all his formative years through graduation from high school in Oak Park, he never identified with his hometown or wrote about it.

Hemingway's biographers emphasize the importance for the young Hemingway of the family summers spent in the northern Michigan woods. There he learned about living in the outdoors and became experienced at hunting, fishing, and hiking. These experiences generated and nurtured the writer's abiding love of the natural world. His looking to nature for personal meaning was likely influenced as well by his exposure to the tradition of Louis Agassiz (encouraged by his mother); Agassiz was an educator interested in promoting a naturalist's proficiency for observing the smallest and slowest workings of nature in order to get a glimpse of the miraculous workings of the Creator. The sacred and restorative power of nature is ubiquitous in Hemingway's stories.

Instead of taking the customary path from high school to college, Hemingway pursued the interest he had developed in high school in writing for the school newspaper and began work in the summer following graduation, in 1917, as a novice reporter for *The Kansas City Star*. The energetic, spare, understated sentences he practiced writing as a journalist later became the trademark style of his fictional writing.

Hemingway's military tour of duty was brief and nontraditional, but he made full use of it in his fiction—most prominently in his second major novel, *A Farewell to Arms* (1929). As Hemingway's stature as an American novelist grew, speculation also grew about exactly what parts of the novel were drawn from autobiographical experience and what parts were the result of research and imagination. All three, as it turns out, contributed to the work, but careful examination of Hemingway's life and this particular novel was undertaken by several Hemingway scholars, notably Carlos Baker, Michael S. Reynolds, Bernard Oldsey, and Charles M. Oliver. Their labors have yielded some clarities.

The United States had been a neutral nation during the first years of World War I, but news about the fighting and the high numbers of casualties was available to American citizens. *The Kansas City Star* ran a series over several days about the devastating retreat from Caporetto in October 1917, and Hemingway signed up for volunteer service with the Red Cross Ambulance Unit in the early months of 1918. (After the United States entered the war in April, he had enlisted in the army and been rejected for poor eyesight.)

Hemingway's Red Cross assignment sent him to the Italian–Austrian front where he drove ambulances for the wounded and delivered mail and goods to the active soldiers. It was during one of these missions, on July 8, 1918, that Hemingway was hit by a mortar shell, but before he became incapacitated by his wounds, he managed to carry a wounded soldier to safety. He was hit again by machine gun fire and taken to the American Red Cross Hospital in Milan where two hundred pieces of shrapnel were removed from his legs. For valorous service, the Italian government twice decorated Hemingway, first, with the Croce di Guerra and second, with the Medaglia d'Argento al Valore Militare.

Hemingway's romance with his nurse, which began during his rehabilitation at the hospital, was the inspiration for the relationship between Frederic Henry and Catherine Barkley. The real-life nurse, Agnes Hannah von Kurowsky, kept a wartime diary. On July 21, she wrote: "Hemingway's birthday, so we all dressed up, & had Gelati on the balcony & played the Victrola. . . . Mr. Seely brought him a large bottle of 5 star Cognac, & they did make merry. I simply can't get to bed early these nights" (quoted in *Dictionary of Literary Biography, Vol. 308: Ernest Hemingway's "A Farewell to Arms,"* 2005: 29). On August 10, she observed: "Hemingway was operated on bright & early. . . . [Everything] went off beautifully." On August 25, she noted: "Now, Ernest Hemingway has a case on me, or thinks he has. He is a dear boy & so cute about it." Two days later, she comes to a conclusion that will later have unhappy consequences for Hemingway: "All I know is 'Ernie' is too fond of me, & speaks in such a desperate way every time I am cool, that I dare not dampen his ardor as long as he is here in the Hospital. Poor Kid, I am sorry for him. . . . Some of the heads have an idea he is very wild and he is—in some respects, but he swears to me in a very honest way that he has always kept clean—& never been bad. I believe it, but the others—oh—no" (ibid). After Hemingway returned to the United States in 1919, he and Agnes exchanged letters (see *Dictionary* 33–35), but she finally rejected his romantic intentions with the assertion that he was too young for her.

Back home in 1919, Hemingway occasionally made public appearances wearing a self-styled uniform similar to that worn by Italian officers. This bold and somewhat odd gesture might be taken as a sign of his now-renowned personality traits: a rebellious impatience with conventional life as defined by Oak Park (or anywhere) and a preoccupation with self-image. (According to some scholars—too numerous to list here—he may also have been hoping to inflate his "war-hero" stature for his hometown.) He was said to have been influenced by the Rough Rider image projected by Teddy Roosevelt during his presidency (1901–09) that came to be associated with high adventure, service to one's country, and a code of honor.

The years 1920 and 1921 were pivotal for Hemingway; he moved to Toronto and took a job as a freelance writer for the *Star;* on a visit to the family summer home he quarreled with his mother who had accused him of "insolence" and reportedly threw him out of the house; and he moved to Chicago where he met Carl Sandburg, Sherwood Anderson, and Hadley Richardson whom he married the next year. In December 1921, he and Hadley sailed for Europe where he planned to support their unconventional life with her trust fund and his writing assignments from the *Star.*

Following the devastation of World War I ("the war [that was to have been] the war to end all wars"), Paris became the European setting for many demoralized American expatriates and others similarly afflicted with postwar disillusionment and alienation. Although Hemingway had enthusiastically embraced his wartime service, the grueling challenges he actually faced made him feel emotionally and intellectually at home in this new community. Celebrated figures in the group included James Joyce, Ezra Pound, and Gertrude Stein; together, they became known (in Stein's famous words) as "the lost generation." Hemingway's 1926 novel, *The Sun Also Rises*, was written during this time and is widely regarded as the classic rendering of this particular mood and moment in American and European cultural history.

Hemingway was an adventurous and migratory person, never staying for long in one place. Based in Paris, he traveled to Switzerland to fish and ski in the Alps, to several sites in Spain for the festivals that ran concurrently with the bullfighting events, and to Italy for a nostalgic return with Hadley. His reporter's assignments took him to dramatic world events such as the Lausanne Peace Conference in 1922 where he interviewed Benito Mussolini, soon to become Italy's fascist dictator, later writing about him (not very presciently) as "Europe's Prize Bluffer."

It was during this time that marital difficulties developed between Hemingway and Hadley, a tense period exacerbated when Hadley, traveling by train to Lausanne to meet her husband at the conference, lost a suitcase filled with three years' worth of his manuscripts. Although a son, John Hadley, was born to the couple in 1923, Hadley divorced Hemingway in 1927. In the same year, he married Pauline Pfeiffer. In 1928, his second son, Patrick, was born, and Hemingway's father committed suicide by shooting himself with a .32 revolver.

Consistent with the existentialist view of life widely adopted by members of the lost generation, Hemingway chose to live adventurously, seeking places where ever-present dangers forced actions and contemplation about what values were worth living for. During the three decades following his first marriage, Hemingway continued to write and publish, but he also traveled almost compulsively and often under dangerous circumstances, suffering more than a normal share of accidents and other maladies. On safari to Kenya he survived two plane crashes in a 24-hour period; his face was clawed by a bear while riding a horse; he was twice injured in car accidents; he went to Madrid to report on the Spanish Civil War; and, in 1942, he volunteered himself and his boat, the *Pilar*, to hunt down German submarines in the Caribbean.

He also divorced two more times (and had more children), finally marrying Martha Welsh in 1946, after an affair in London where she was working, as he would later, as a war correspondent. By this time, Hemingway had traveled to Cuba and bought a home—Finca Vigía ("Lookout Farm")—which remained his primary residence for the rest of his life. In 1958, he rented, and a year later bought, a house in Ketchum, Idaho, and was living there when the dictator Fulgencio Batista was overthrown and Fidel Castro took power.

Hemingway's writing and publishing career was successful by any standard of judgment. He received accolades from many fronts, was emulated by younger writers, and, in 1954, after the publication of *The Old Man and the Sea* (1952), was awarded the Nobel Prize for Literature. He was also a charismatic public figure. He was pictured on the covers and pages of *Life* and *Time* magazines; Hollywood adapted his novels and stories into 14 movies; and Archibald MacLeish famously said that the "only [other] person [he had ever known] who could exhaust the oxygen in a room the way Ernest could just by coming into it was Franklin Delano Roosevelt" (quoted in Scott Donaldson's *By Force of Will: The Life and Art of Ernest Hemingway*, p. 2).

Despite these successes, Hemingway had been suffering bouts of depression intermittently through the years; they became more debilitating later in life and were exacerbated by feelings of paranoia and various physical ailments. His wife remained attentive and loyal throughout, but battling the worst effects of these afflictions became more of an effort and, finally, his major preoccupation. Donaldson discusses multiple ways during this period that Hemingway expressed suicidal impulses and fantasies (see pp. 282–290, 303–305). During the last year of his life, Hemingway found himself physically and mentally unable to make words appear on paper. He was twice hospitalized at the Mayo Clinic where he received electroshock treatments. "Perhaps," writes Donaldson, "what he had accomplished—one of the enduring literary accomplishments of the twentieth century—could no longer offer solace to a man who could only think of what he could no longer do" (305). On the morning of July 2, 1961, in his Ketchum home, Hemingway shot himself with his double-barreled shotgun and died. Official expressions of sorrow came later in the day from the White House, the Vatican, and the Kremlin.

The Story Behind the Story

In August 1914 World War I began; in May 1915, after a period of neutrality, Italy entered the war on the side of the Allies and made advances against the forces of Austria–Hungary. The American president, Woodrow Wilson, was re-elected in 1916 with a campaign promise to keep the United States out of the war; a few months later, in April 1917, Wilson announced that the United States would join the war effort on the side of the Allies—a necessary decision, he famously declared, to "make the world safe for democracy." In October of the same year, Austrian and German troops took the offensive and forced the Italian troops into a disastrous retreat from the village of Caporetto. During this retreat in 1917, hundreds of thousands of Italian soldiers deserted, were captured, or lost their lives. On Armistice Day, November 11, 1918, the war ended for the Western forces. Ten million soldiers had been killed and 22 million wounded.

It became known as the Great War.

During the period of American neutrality, U.S. citizens had access to information about the massive suffering experienced by the Allies—privations deepened by the length of time required to transport the wounded in horse-drawn carts from the fields to the hospitals. One response, in November 1914, came from the American novelist Henry James, who publicly cited the generosity of his countrymen and -women and urged everyone to find a way to aid the wounded. As a result of this and other appeals, the American Volunteer Motor-Ambulance Corps was established.

Ernest Hemingway was 18 years old and a high school graduate when he signed on to work for the American Red Cross in the European theater of the war. He was sent to northern Italy where, for just one month during the summer of 1918, he worked as an ambulance driver until he was wounded by a mortar shell. *A Farewell to Arms*, begun in March 1928 and published in September 1929, cannot accurately be called autobiographical but it contains autobiographical elements, and it received high praise for its accuracy and realism from soldiers who had had long and substantial involvement in the war. Two scholars, in particular—Michael S. Reynolds (*Hemingway's First War: The Making of "A Farewell to Arms,"* 1976) and Charles M. Oliver (*Ernest Hemingway's "A Farewell to Arms: A Documentary Volume*, 2005)—have published their own extensive findings on the research Hemingway undertook to be able to write about the geography, seasonal changes, and specific events in the war with convincing accuracy.

Hemingway's single month of noncombat service was not his only direct experience with the war, however. Like Frederic Henry, he also fell in love with a wartime nurse. With what turned out to be more than two hundred pieces of shrapnel in his legs, Hemingway was taken to the American hospital in Milan and operated on twice. Among the nursing staff at the hospital was Agnes Hannah von Kurowsky, who became the model for Catherine Barkley. During the months of writing *Farewell*, Hemingway was reportedly so caught up by the events he was narrating that he became removed from the events occurring in his own life. An exception was Pauline's prolonged and difficult labor in giving birth to Patrick—a harrowing event that figured prominently in the novel.

Hemingway began his composition of *Farewell* in March 1928, two years after the publication of *The Sun Also Rises*. His first working titles were *The World's Room* and *Nights and Forever* followed by *Hill of Heaven* and *A Separate Peace*. Of the more than 30 alternative titles considered, another telling option was *World Enough and Time*, an appropriate use of the famous line from Andrew Marvell's poem, "To His Coy Mistress," about an impatient lover reminding his lover of the brevity of youth and time.

Learning about the various titles Hemingway considered for his novel is one way to get at the author's emotion and perspective for the story he wanted to tell. Another is to keep in mind the impact of the war and its aftermath. In the words of critic Sandra Whipple Spanier, it is important to remember that

World War I was a mechanized horror unprecedented in human history, a war . . . that exacted casualties hideous in their nature and number—and for no reason that anyone could understand. . . . [Great] engagements like Verdun had proved nothing except that a million men could die in a single battle without changing so much as a front line. ("Hemingway's Unknown Soldier," *New Essays on "A Farewell to Arms,"* 83)

A cultural shift in attitude—the beginnings of modernism or the modernist outlook—was a direct consequence of the war. An entire generation of thoughtful, educated, formerly idealistic men and women in Europe and the United States experienced a collapse of the traditional verities of honor, service, patriotism, and commitment to country. Cynicism was stronger than aspiration, meaninglessness and alienation were more commonly experienced than hopeful and righteous purposefulness. In what Robert Penn Warren called (in his introduction to the 1949 edition of *Farewell*) the "God-abandoned world of modernity," meaning and value were the responsibility of each individual. Hemingway described this world and the "lost generation" inhabiting it in his earlier novel, *The Sun Also Rises* (1926); he was a member of this generation and he was writing *Farewell* from this perspective. In his introduction to the collection of war stories, *Men at War* (1942), Hemingway ascribed to a soldier the capacity required of every thinking person living in this time period: "learning to suspend [one's] imagination and live completely in the very second of the present moment with no before and no after . . ." (17). This capacity is one component of the Hemingway "code" of honorable behavior and is characteristic of the worldview associated with modernism and existentialism.

In February 1929, Maxwell Perkins, Hemingway's editor at Scribner's, offered $16,000 for the rights to serialize the novel in *Scribner's Magazine*. Hemingway was happy with the offer—an impressive sum for the times—but not happy to learn that a few words and brief passages needed to be omitted because their language or content was deemed disturbing and offensive for some likely readers. Hemingway, indignant, resisted but later relented, to little avail as it turned out, because the magazine itself was banned in Boston, after the first installment appeared in its June issue.

The deletions, apparently, had been insufficient to placate some sensibilities: certain readers were offended by Hemingway's use of "rough language" in conversations between soldiers; others were shocked by the graphic details in the scenes involving childbirth and the retreat of the Italian soldiers; some disapproved of the author's sympathetic treatment of Henry's desertion from combat; and the biggest group of offended readers opposed any favorable depiction of sexual love between an unmarried man and woman.

Hemingway's censors did not go unanswered. Many critics publicly praised the novel's beauty and clarity and insisted its message was essentially moral. There was also the argument that the then-current literary trends in modernism and naturalism required that novelists describe life realistically, as it actually sounded and appeared. Hemingway's artistic integrity compelled him to insist on publishing the novel intact, and when it first appeared on September 27, 1929, it was well received both popularly and critically. As it turned out, then as now, negative publicity begets extra attention. The spectacle of policemen confiscating copies of the serialized version of the novel from the newsstands in Boston increased sales of the book. Even with the stock market crash in October, Scribner's made six reprintings in the first three months for a total of 79,251 copies sold. In Italy, however, in spite of Hemingway's public avowal that *A Farewell to Arms* was not written to criticize Italy or the Italian military, the novel was banned by Mussolini as was a later movie version.

The first film adaptation was antiquated, slow moving, in black and white; it was released in 1932 and starred Gary Cooper and Helen Hayes. The second appeared in Technicolor in 1957 and starred Rock Hudson and Jennifer Jones. A third movie, *In Love and War* (1996), starring Sandra Bullock and Chris O'Donnell, attempts (badly, according to most critics) to portray Hemingway's own war-zone and wartime romance experiences that he drew from for his novel.

Over the years since their publication, *A Farewell to Arms* and *The Sun Also Rises* have competed for favorite status among popular and critical readers alike. Several variables have been influential. *Sun* was appreciated by Vietnam War–era readers for the way it rendered the demoralizing and alienating effect of apparently senseless combat. *Farewell* recalls for readers with war experience the harshness and poignancy of their own tours of duty.

Responses to the character of Catherine have altered dramatically from one period to another—changes that reflect evolving views about female characters in literature. Some early critics divided Hemingway's women into stereotypical categories; for example, in the words of the influential critic, Edmund Wilson, Hemingway's female creations were either "submissive . . . Anglo-Saxon women that make his heroes such perfect mistresses" or "American bitches of the most soul-destroying sort" (*Atlantic* 164, July 1939: 36–46). Sandra Whipple Spanier notes in "Hemingway's Unknown Soldier" (76) that Wilson was the first critic to identify Catherine as the first character in Hemingway's oeuvre to reflect and absorb the author's alleged misogyny.

In the 1970s and 1980s, *Farewell* fell out of favor in schools and colleges because of many teachers' fears of having to encounter or deflect feminist objections to the perceived passivity of Catherine's character. In 1976, critic Judith Fetterley published an essay ("Hemingway's 'Resentful Cryptogram'") in the *Journal of Popular Culture* (Summer 1976: 203–214) that signaled the impassioned anti-Hemingway sentiment coming from feminist thinkers. She argued that Catherine suffers because she has complicated Lieutenant Henry's life by getting pregnant, and she and her baby must die because Hemingway cannot or does not want to imagine a man's life that involves commitment and adult responsibility. Another feminist critic, Joyce Wexler, reads the same novel and sees Catherine as a mature woman who knowingly and bravely moves to salvage her life with a new love and who, far more than the adolescent Frederic, understands what few choices there are to create a life marked with meaning and integrity.

Hemingway did not know how to end his novel. In critic Bernard Oldsey's documentation of the author's lengthy and laborious writing and rewriting of the novel, he lists 39 different conclusions that were considered. Not very succinctly, these can be summarized as (1) "The *Nada* Ending" in which the author reminds us of the perennial truth that everyone must die someday and that it was simply Catherine and her baby's time to die; (2) "The Fitzgerald Ending": "the world . . . kills the very good and the very gentle and the very brave impartially"; (3) "The Religious Ending," which notices the "wisdom of the priest . . . who has always loved God and so is happy . . . [and asks] but how much is wisdom and how much is luck to be . . . born that way?"; (4) "The Live Baby Ending": "I could tell about the boy . . . [but] he does not belong in this story"; and (5) "The Morning-After Ending" that prolongs Frederic Henry's suffering by tracing his steps to the hotel where he finally and fitfully falls asleep and awakens to the realization that nothing will ever be the same again. (See Oldsey 101–110.)

The following is from George Plimpton's interview with Hemingway, which first appeared in the *Paris Review* in 1958 (reproduced in Oldsey, p. 70):

> "How much re-writing do you do?"
>
> "It depends. I re-wrote the ending of *Farewell to Arms*, the last page of it, thirty-nine times before I was satisfied."
>
> "Was there some technical problem there? What was it had you stumped?"
>
> "Getting the words right."

Like all writers, Hemingway was forced to find his way to the end of his own novel, leaving present-day readers with a complex work whose elements and implications are still being elucidated and debated.

List of Characters

Frederic Henry, the protagonist and narrator, is an American ambulance driver serving in northern Italy during World War I. Without religion or patriotic zeal, he has only his love for Catherine to sustain him. As his experiences in love and war deepen, he grows in awareness and allows himself to feel life more intensely. Most readers come to admire Henry for his ambulance service, his devotion to Catherine, and his willingness to acknowledge his failings, but other readers find him passive, irresponsible, and self-absorbed.

Catherine Barkley is the British nurse working in Italy during World War I who catches the casual and then sustained attention of Lieutenant Frederic Henry, the American, who is also in Italy working for the Italian war effort. Catherine has been traumatized by the sudden death of her fiancé who was killed in the battle at the Somme in France. Readers and critics differ widely in their understanding of Catherine, with adjectives ranging from "pathetically passive" to "heroic" (in the sense Hemingway's code entails).

The Priest is one of those rare characters whose presence calls everyone—some more uncomfortably than others—to an awareness of higher purpose and meaning while at the same time remaining likable and worthy of respect. The teasing he receives from some of the men about his celibacy does not alter his good-natured and compassionate interactions with them—perhaps because he knows how uncomfortable and frightened the men are. The priest's view of the war evolves as the novel does; he finds it increasingly difficult to justify the immense and widespread suffering he witnesses. Most importantly, the priest provides the novel's definition of love—"When you love you wish to do things for"—which stands in contrast to what is "only passion and lust." The priest has the greatest influence on Lieutenant Henry who is, at first, respectfully dismissive of the priest's views but becomes increasingly attentive to his presence and insight.

Lieutenant Rinaldi, the Italian doctor, works tirelessly and skillfully at the front. Playful and irreverent, he seems to be always dodging the big questions. He lives at a frenetic pace, moving among his work responsibilities, the pleasures of alcohol, and his numerous but brief sexual encounters that result in his contracting syphilis. Inordinately but not awkwardly fond of Frederic, Rinaldi calls him his "best friend and . . . war brother." Underneath the comradely banter, Rinaldi's loneliness seems obvious.

Helen Ferguson is a Scottish nurse who is ambivalent about Frederic Henry and protective of her friend Catherine, but she enables their relationship to develop. She gives hints of having experienced a past love affair that ended badly, but she keeps her life private, and we do not learn anything more about her.

Miss Van Campen, head nurse at the Milan hospital, is an experienced medical professional who is also relentlessly authoritarian and difficult to like. She and Frederic clash from their first meeting. Hemingway's distaste for authoritarian women is well known, but his portrayal seems excessively unfair and cruel for a woman with huge responsibilities who must labor under harsh conditions.

Gage and **Walker** are also nurses at the hospital. Walker seems overwhelmed to the point of helplessness; Gage is helpful and harmlessly flirtatious.

Manera, **Passini**, **Gavuzzi**, and **Gordini** are ambulance drivers with Lieutenant Henry. Passini is killed by a trench bomb; Gordini and Henry are wounded at the same time.

Ettore Moretti, an Italian who was raised in the United States, is an officer in the Italian Army and an acquaintance of Frederic Henry. He is preoccupied with his promotions and boastful about his wounds and medals, which Catherine finds distasteful and boring. Ettore shows no signs of having an inner life, no place for doubt or ambivalence. He seems callous about killing enemy soldiers and, if the pay were better, he would fight for the U.S. Army.

Count Greffi is an elderly cultured gentleman who befriends Frederic in Stresa and looks forward to their conversations. Before Frederic leaves with Catherine for Switzerland, the two have an important talk about death and one's purpose for living.

Piani, **Bonello**, and **Aymo** are, with Lieutenant Henry, the last of the ambulance drivers to leave the front after the order comes to begin the retreat. Aymo is killed, and Bonello deserts when they leave the main route of retreat to seek a safer way to Udine. Henry is particularly saddened to lose the companionship of Aymo.

Summary and Analysis

Book One

Chapter I begins with a classic example of the writing style for which Hemingway is known: lean, understated, evocative, spare, and without emotion. The author has positioned the reader "in a house, in a village that looked across the river and the plain to the mountains" (*A Farewell to Arms*, New York: Charles Scribner's Sons, 1929, 1957, p. 3)—a kind of lookout point that effectively compels feelings of detachment. Whatever emotion is evoked here flows from the reader's association with the imagined scene, especially with the soldiers marching at too great of a distance to be identified as individuals.

Nearly every commentator points to the opening paragraph for its "painterly" quality and to the brief opening chapter for its stark and depersonalized picture of war. One of these, Mark P. Ott, in his study of Hemingway's love of open water and other wild places in nature, observes about the first paragraph that in the use of "contrasting structures of the dry leaves and the swiftly moving river, the repetition of the words 'leaves,' 'dust,' and 'white,' ... the movement of the troops ... [and] the perspective of looking over the plain to the mountains, ... Hemingway was trying to capture the essence of Cezanne's paintings" (*A Sea of Change* 67).

The biblical reminder of human fate moving "from dust to dust" is clearly present in the images of endless dust and falling leaves. The sudden appearance of the king to get a quick and relatively risk-free glimpse of how the war effort was going ("very badly") is another reminder of the human condition; namely, the arbitrary assignment of power to some while not to others. In the end, however, as Hemingway scholar Carlos Baker writes, "Into the dust is where the troops are going—some of them soon, all of them eventually" (*Hemingway: The Writer as Artist* 95).

A year passes between Chapter I and Chapter II, and the authorial perspective remains distant; no one yet has been identified by name. The protagonist has made casual friendships with the other officers and takes part in their lighthearted banter. He does not, however, join in the sexually explicit teasing of the reverent and good-natured priest, nor does he offer any opinions about the war or Italian opera. He is an observer, not yet touched personally by the war. The arrival of snow signals a seasonal suspension of hostilities, leaving the soldiers with only the question of where to go on leave. To the American far from home, the priest offers hospitality with his family whose members partake of the clear, cold, pure life of the mountains. The officers propose yet another visit to the nearest brothel. Neither love nor religion stirs the American; he says a respectful goodnight to the priest and half-heartedly follows the officers out the door. A feature of earlier and more primitive forms of warfare seen here is the alternating periods of active fighting with respites for more civilized life.

The story intensifies in Chapter III. All the sentences are in the past tense (as they have been from the beginning), and yet more time has passed. The American is telling his story slowly and deliberately, as if feeling a need to understand each detail. This is how one proceeds when seeking perspective and resolution about a significant event in the past. As the reader advances through the story, it is important to notice how the protagonist changes as he expands his story.

In the room Frederic returns to after his leave, all of his war-related items are neatly arranged—the horrifying gasmask next to the comforting blanket. His effusively affectionate and high-spirited roommate, the lieutenant and surgeon Rinaldi, greets him with news of all the girls recently arrived at the front and an announcement that he has just fallen in love with Miss Barkley, a beautiful English nurse he is already fantasizing about marrying. In the next breath, he lists the extraneous medical conditions he has been dealing with in his patients: frostbite, jaundice, gonorrhea and others he categorizes—perhaps because they are insufficiently serious to deserve his surgeon's skill—as not quite the "real" wounds of war.

The American lieutenant tells himself he had intended during his leave to visit with the priest's family but ended up indulging in the transient pleasures of alcohol and impersonal sex. The awkwardness he feels greeting the priest on his return signifies his ambivalence and embarrassment around the kind of pure and formal religious belief the priest represents. He writes, "[The priest] had always known what I did not know and what, when I learned it, I was always able to forget. But I did not know that then, although I learned it later" (14). This cryptic statement indicates that something will occur later in the story that the narrator knows and values.

Chapter IV provides evidence of the American's detachment from the war effort: not only is he not European, much of his work with the ambulances—concealing their position from the enemy, for example—gives only "a false feeling of soldiering" (17). He also seems, for some reason, willing to admit that "the whole thing [the ambulance corps] seemed to run better while [he] was away" (17).

In their surprisingly direct and intimate first exchange, he and Catherine reveal a telling difference between them: he is impulsive and fatalistic about his choices—in this instance, about why an American would be driving an ambulance for Italian soldiers he does not know (he was in Italy and spoke some Italian)—and she plays with the notion that everything has an explanation ("I was brought up to think there was") but quickly retreats from disagreement, as if she were merely testing him. This tiny revelation of difference makes her seem older and perhaps more willing to be reflective. Then, as she reveals the loss of her former love, we sense why: she was once romantic and hopeful—"[I thought] he might come to the hospital where I was [with] a sabre cut [or some other picturesque wound]"—but instead he was brought to the hospital "[after] they blew him all to bits" (20). Catherine has seen dreams turn to nightmares, life into death—brutally, and at a relatively young age.

In Chapter V, after a description of the way the landscape is ravaged by war with roads carved through pristine woods and little towns reduced to rubble, we see in Frederic and Catherine's next exchanges how war changes courtship and love between a man and woman, accelerating intimacy and coercing it into a cheap seduction. Catherine resists the "nurse's-evening-off aspect" of his advances with a sudden slap to his face but quickly succumbs to his advances as if she were not quite in control of herself. He is ready to move forward without much consideration and wants to put thoughts of war out of their minds—"Let's drop the war"—to which she, with more experience, responds with the more knowing remark, "[there's] no place to drop it" (26). Later, back in the room, Rinaldi jests and seems unbothered that his roommate has just laid claim to the object of his infatuation. For some of the novel's characters, trapped in such a harrowing situation, nothing can be taken seriously, nothing can be imagined or treated as permanent.

Chapter VI brings back the reality of imminent war—its absurdity and barbarity both: the toilet paper pistol, the pistol too powerful to be useful, and the English gas mask to protect against the cyanide that mercilessly killed hundreds of thousands of men and cavalry horses. Love, in this chapter, is a pleasantly distracting game for Henry, but, for Catherine, it is a desperate but deliberate fantasy. It is not clear to what extent she is "out of her mind" with grief for her lost fiancé. She certainly expressed a degree of mental imbalance or wish fulfillment when she insists that Frederic speak to her as if he is her lost love come back: "Say, 'I've come back to Catherine in the night.'" Frederic confesses he thought "she was a little bit crazy" (31). Something in this interaction causes him to pause and remember a time when he thought that, in a game like bridge, one plays for money whereas in the "love game," instead of playing with cards, you use words, pretending you are playing to win something, playing for stakes. Writing after the fact, he can say plainly and also ironically: "Nobody had mentioned what the stakes were" (32). "The stakes" are what his story is about.

Chapter VII advances two important ideas in the novel. The first is the ongoing detachment of Frederic Henry. Alone while waiting for the wounded to arrive, Henry can find nothing to think about; later, thinking about some friends or relatives back home, he can think of nothing to write about. Fear is unreal to him, as well, "no more dangerous to [him] . . . than war in the movies"; he expects to escape death or injury because the "war did not have anything to do with [him]" (38). This naïve view was not Hemingway's; the writer is depicting his character as one who has not yet come to terms with the reality rather than the idea of war. This respect for the tangible and concrete is a mark of Hemingway's writing. Another sign of Frederic's inexperience is that only at the end of the evening when he is drunk and it is too late to visit Catherine does he acknowledge or even notice that he has an emotional life. "I was feeling lonely and hollow," he observes (43).

A second theme is the randomness of war illustrated when a nonfatally wounded soldier comes close to getting aid from a sympathetic ambulance driver but is found first by his own regiment and sent back to the front. This incident also demonstrates the desperate art of feigning injury.

The chapter also contains a brief and poignant excursion into the human imagination; Henry has a fantasy—in step-by-step progression—of magically disappearing with Catherine from the war and ending up in a Milan hotel room with a bottle of *capri bianca*. "That was how it ought to be," he thinks. In this novel and others, Hemingway takes many opportunities to dramatize the difference between what is imagined and what actually occurs and must be endured.

The long-anticipated resumption of hostilities finally takes place in Chapter VIII. As Frederic heads toward the action in the ambulance, he briefly re-enacts two ancient rituals of wartime: he says a hurried goodbye to his lover and accepts a protective talisman—in this case, a St. Anthony's necklace from Catherine. Hemingway's details about the geography of this area of Italy are so precise that someone unfamiliar with the region could retrace the path of the convoys just from his account. Each bend in the road with its subsequent view, each curve of each river, the places where the water is smooth and slow moving or rushing and turbulent over the pebbles, all these are details of a beloved and well-known landscape. Hemingway did not know all of Italy's various regions, but what he knew he remembered and loved; what he did not know, he researched to make accurate.

Another ancient ritual associated with wartime is enacted in Chapter IX: calculating strategies to end the war and comparing plans of action and outcomes to determine the best that can be hoped for and the worst that must otherwise be endured. "If everybody would not attack" is one solution proposed; another is to fight on because defeat is worse than war. No one uttering these ideas has the power to bring them about, and there is no resolving which ideas are the best ones. Still, this is far from idle talk: the participants are sitting in a dugout, temporarily sheltered from artillery and gunfire. Hemingway had his own ideas about the war that he develops as the novel proceeds. It is hard, however, to improve on the following logic:

> Did you see all the far mountains today? Do you think we could take all them too? Only if the Austrians stop fighting. One side must stop fighting. Why don't we stop fighting? If they come down into Italy they will get tired and go away. They have their own country. (53)

What follows this interlude of reasonableness is the brutal unreasonableness of war: the maiming and killing of soldiers while they are trying to fortify themselves with a primitive meal of cold pasta, cheese, and wine that has gone bad. Like Hemingway, Frederic is wounded in the process of delivering food. Also like the author, Frederic comes to the aid of a wounded soldier before accepting medical attention. Passini is the wounded one; eventually, in great agony, he succumbs to his wounds and dies. Frederic reports having had what is now called an out-of-body experience at the moment of the shell's first impact, but he returns to life, seriously, but not fatally, wounded. Frederic's demeanor as he is being tended to and transported following his injury is exactly what is expected of a Hemingway hero: no complaining, no outward show of feeling pain, no undue attention requested. There will be other examples later in the novel.

A separate issue relevant to the historical period comes to light in this chapter. Italian immigrants to the United States at this time were cast in the role of disapproving stereotypes, but there is no sense that Frederic is identified with these anti-Italian sentiments or in any way held responsible for them. Jeffrey A. Schwarz makes this point in his essay, "Who's the foreigner now?" Not only are the Italian officers and soldiers deferential to Frederic both before and after his wounding, they behave in nonstereotypical ways. Schwarz points out how approvingly Frederic speaks about the Italians when he and Catherine are at the races in Milan and he is contemplating his desertion. Speculating that Hemingway may have been deliberately correcting some of the negative stereotypes, Schwarz writes: "The fact that Frederic/Hemingway makes a point of noting that there are 'good,' 'brave,' 'calm,' and 'sensible' Italians . . . seems significant given the rampant American prejudice against Italians at the time when Hemingway was writing *A Farewell to Arms*" (*Hemingway's Italy*, 2006, 113).

In his bed at the field hospital in Chapter X, Frederic is baffled when informed he will be awarded a medal for, as he puts it, getting "blown up while . . . [eating] cheese" (66). Genuine heroism is a reality of warfare, but careless or manipulative use of language produces an inflated rhetoric which a genuine soldier—or Hemingway hero—would find embarrassing. Frederic protests but to no avail, and his friend Rinaldi misses the irony, but in the affectionate male banter between them and name-calling, the moment passes.

Passages such as those found in Chapter XI generate a range of interpretive responses. Pamela A. Boker, a critic writing from a psychoanalytic perspective, argues that Frederic Henry—like other American male figures created by American writers Hemingway, Twain, and Melville—is acting out an adolescent and regressive retreat from complexity and the responsibilities associated with maturity and adulthood. She cites Frederic's hesitancy to fully engage in the war's meaning and his quickness to deflect any notion of heroism as signs of a failure to come to terms with the loss of idealism associated with the emergence of modernist thinking. As evidence for an unconscious longing for regression, she notes the pleasure Frederic has lying in bed imagining returning to his childhood: "It was like being put to bed after early supper" (71). She writes:

Wounding facilitates the Hemingway hero's regressive fantasy for unconditional love. It is not the wound itself, therefore, but this unconscious desire for love that may be identified as the repressed, which continually returns in Hemingway's fiction. (*The Grief Taboo in American Literature* 198)

The priest is Frederic's second visitor. In contrast to Rinaldi, he comes with doubts about the war, which Frederic does not yet share, and thoughtful gifts requiring consideration and effort. Making these considerations and efforts is what the priest is talking about when he tells Henry during their awkwardly intimate conversation: "When you love you wish to do things for. You wish to sacrifice for. You wish to serve" (75). This definition of love stands in contrast to the "passion and lust" most of the others (Rinaldi, in particular) are seeking with "the newest girls," and Frederic admits that he does not know what the priest is talking about: "I don't love." At this point in the novel, Frederic seems to think he is not missing out on anything important—he is happy, he is always happy, he insists—but he shows some curiosity in the priest's sentiments.

The priest is a man of his word; he is sincere and not a hypocrite. Even his smallest gestures appear to flow from a generosity of feeling: when Frederic persuades him to share a glass of the bottle of vermouth the priest has brought as a gift, he immediately thinks of returning with more. This conversation about different kinds of love will inform later developments in the novel, as will the equally awkward and important exchange of ideas between them about loving God. In the course of the visit, the priest inadvertently exposes the suffering he has been enduring when picked on about "the girls." Although consistently good natured about being relentlessly teased by the others, he expresses the wish to Frederic that after the war he can return to "[his] country" where "it is understood that a man may love God" (74). Frederic falls asleep reflecting on what he knows about the priest's country; as is common in Hemingway's stories, the best and most honest conversations between men happen in wild and pristine landscapes.

Chapter XII gives a brief glimpse into the mundane realities of wartime. Frederic is visited again by Rinaldi and the major; they get drunk and engage in amiable banter. Frederic has a hard time being transported to Milan where—Rinaldi has happily informed him—he is to be taken to an American hospital and cared for by British nurses, including Catherine. On the way he drinks to dull the pain, gets sick, and then drinks some more. This chapter closes Book One in which the worst, the best, and the mundane aspects of warfare have been briefly but effectively dramatized.

Book Two

Hemingway critic Carlos Baker calls attention to two opposing sets of values in the novel with separate associated activities and geography; he refers to these divisions as "Home" and "Not-Home":

> The Home-concept . . . is associated with the mountains; with dry-cold weather; with peace and quiet; with love, dignity, health, happiness, and the good life; and with worship or at least consciousness of God. The Not-Home concept is associated with low-lying plains; with rain and fog; with obscenity, indignity, disease, suffering, nervousness, war and death; and with irreligion. (*Hemingway: The Writer as Artist* 102)

Except for the priest's description of, and Frederic's reveries about, Abruzzi, Book One has been mainly about Not-Home. Book Two shifts the focus to Home.

In Chapter XIII Frederic learns that, inconveniently for everyone, he is the first patient to arrive at the hospital, and his arrival was unexpected. While he waits for his treatment, he passes the time looking out the window and flirting with—or annoying—the nurses.

When, in Chapter XIV, Catherine arrives, Frederic has an epiphany: "When I saw her I was in love with her. Everything turned over inside of me" (95). Later, after a brief and "stolen" interlude of love, Catherine leaves, but the epiphany continues: "God knows I had not wanted to fall in love with her. I had not wanted to fall in love with anyone. But God knows I had . . ." (97). This change follows Frederic's near-death experience. Three doctors attend to him in Chapter XV, and, although he trusts no one, he chooses the most jovial of the doctors, and the only one willing, to operate immediately on the knee.

In Chapter XVI, Catherine and Frederic enjoy a lover's tryst the night before his operation—a pleasure no doubt forbidden in the hospital, possibly medically unwise, and certainly likely to put the more authoritarian nurses into a rage. Whatever the consequences, they are compelled to seek each other out, caught up in the first stage of love, giddy and earnest and grave, all at once. Readers, however, may already notice two worrisome flaws in this relationship. Frederic is still able to lie to her (when he perceives the issue to be unimportant), and Catherine is quick to sacrifice her sense of self to this union ("There isn't any me any more," she tells him). Romantic love seems to involve losing one's identity. This issue has received the attention of many readers, among them, many prominent feminist critics.

Frederic's surgery goes well, but he spends less time in immediate recovery with the other nurses than he does with Catherine because her nighttime visits have been noticed, and she has become increasing tired as well. One of the nurses, Helen Ferguson, is friendly to Henry but protective of Catherine and warns against her having a war baby. The two have a conversation full of foreboding.

"Will you come to our wedding, Fergy?"
"You'll never get married."
"We will."
"No you won't."
"Why not?"
"You'll fight before you'll marry."
"We never fight."
"You've time yet."

"We don't fight."

"You'll die then. Fight or die. That's what people do. They don't marry."

Whatever painful memory stands behind this resigned sadness, Fergy chooses not to reveal it.

Hemingway is known for his relish of the simpler pleasures of life. In Chapter XVIII, as Frederic awaits full recuperation, he recalls many of these as he and Catherine enjoy their summertime interlude of idleness and budding love. There are the wines (dry white capri, barbera, sweet white, and freesia that might or might not taste of strawberries) and the food ("ham and lettuce sandwiches and anchovy sandwiches made of very tiny brown glazed rolls . . . as long as your finger") and one memorable detail of physical intimacy—Catherine loosening her long hair so that beneath it Frederic has the "feeling of [being] inside a tent or behind a [waterfall]" (117–118). We also see what may be another example of Hemingway's effort to offset American anti-Italian feeling when George the headwaiter at the Gran Italia restaurant lends 100 lire to Frederic who has run short.

Frederic and Catherine, still in the first flush of love, discuss marriage, but Catherine dismisses the idea as risky—"[the authorities] would send [her] away"—and unnecessary—"We're [already] married" (119). The reader might naturally be curious about both the suddenness and the ardor of Catherine's commitment to Frederic. Her grief for her lost love seemed real enough, but with Frederic's arrival it becomes ephemeral. The reader is left pondering the nature of the romantic love that both are declaring. Catherine had previously described her love as a state of rapturous merging, a union with Frederic so engulfing as to lose all sense of separateness. In this chapter, romantic love is equated with religion or, as Catherine says: "You're my religion. You're all I've got" (120). During this time, the lovers are devoted to their own utter and complete happiness. There seems to be, however, a desperate quality to Catherine's eagerness to be happy: "Do let's please just be happy" (121).

In Chapter XIX, while passing the time waiting for Catherine to get off duty, Frederic meets some acquaintances on a Milan sidewalk, most memorably, Ettore Moretti, an Italian raised in the United States and now serving in his country's army. Frederic calls him "a legitimate war hero," but Ettore is a bit of an exhibitionist, bragging about his scars and medals. Catherine finds him boring. Hemingway explicitly admired men who endured what was asked of them without calling attention to the effort or suffering involved. Catherine also has no interest in medals or promotions or any kind of official status—like being married—because, like so many of her generation who are living through what seems like the worst of times, she sees value only in the meanings that one makes for oneself. She is part of the culture of modernism that views the traditional values as unsustainable and untrustworthy.

In the evening, Catherine confesses to fearing the rain, because she frequently pictures herself dead when it is raining. The dread of anticipated loss is inextricably a part of romantic love; but the association of death with rain is one Hemingway has already established in the first pages of the novel. The lovers dismiss their fears as "nonsense" and go to bed.

Disinterestedly, Frederic and Catherine bet on horseraces with several acquaintances, and it quickly becomes clear that the races are rigged. Even winning horses seem to lose money for their backers. Hemingway especially detested the corruption of performance sports like bullfighting and horseracing by gambling or other seductions, but he was drawn to many kinds of sporting events and liked writing about what he knew. Of this scene, critic Michael Reynolds suggests that the rigged races at the San Siro track are emblematic of life itself as viewed from the postwar perspective; namely, that "life is a fixed race in which there are no winners." He goes on:

Support must be given and taken when chance permits, for against the backdrop of the Italian front, [Catherine and Frederic] are but inconsequential specks whose lives will be missed by no one but each other. Both are war wounded, and both use each other, in the best sense, to bind those wounds. (*"A Farewell to Arms": Doctors in the House of Love,"* Cambridge Companion to Hemingway, 1996: 121)

In wartime, peaceful interludes are short lived, and, as expected, news comes, in Chapter XXI, of many losses for the Italians and no progress at the front. In romantic love, also, bliss is unsustainable. With trepidation, Catherine tells Frederic that she is three months pregnant. The Frederic Henry who responds to this news is more aware and more mature than the somewhat cynical lieutenant of the earlier chapters who enjoyed drinking with the officers, did not object to their teasing of the priest, and unthinkingly followed them when they left for the brothels. Here, the prospect of his being responsible for a child changes everything, and the reader senses this transformation beginning when Frederic says, "We were quiet awhile and did not talk" (145). Once again, Frederic presents himself in a less than flattering way when he confesses to being about as brave as a ballplayer batting at .230, in other words, not impressive or worthy of emulation.

Many critics have commented on Catherine's manner in these passages, especially her question to Frederic, "[You] don't feel trapped?", and his answer, "You always feel trapped biologically." The meaning of this exchange depends on one's belief about free will and whether a purpose for living exists outside the realm of human meaning. Frederic could say he felt duty-bound to a religious or civil authority, but it is to nature only that he feels connected. The biological determinants are the ones that matter; one's destiny unfolds according to rules over which one has no control. This emphasis in thinking, called naturalism in literature, is a common component of the modernist view of the world. About this passage, Mark P. Ott writes, "Nature, not free will, according to naturalist critics, controls the destiny of this couple" (Ott 61).

Strong reactions are also registered about Catherine's apparently complete submission to Frederic; her concern is whether he feels trapped but not whether she does. She also appears apologetic, as if one person could be responsible for a pregnancy. Discussions on these topics are numerous and easy to find. What is indisputable is that sooner or later the euphoric rush of romantic love is checked; when this happens, other considerations and perspectives become unavoidable and imperative. Love has consequences and its complexities.

In Chapter XXII, the long-standing animosity between Frederic and Miss Van Campen escalates to a face-off over her discovery of Frederic's capacious consumption of alcohol. Empty bottles once filled with cognac and vermouth have been snuck out of the hospital room, but these and the other remaining ones have not escaped the eyes of the head nurse. Hemingway and Frederic are hard on Miss Van Campen and disrespectful, as well, exploiting her status as an unmarried and childless woman. This kind of attitude helped to ignite the feminist hostility to Hemingway that began to coalesce in the 1960s and 1970s. Hemingway disliked authoritarian women, especially those who seem, as Miss Van Campen does here, to enjoy "punishing" men, in this case, Frederic, who is not permitted to take his leave with Catherine. He has three weeks before returning to the front.

In Chapter XXIII, with Frederic about to return to the battlefield, he and Catherine spend their last hours together walking around Milan in a cold and unpleasant rain. Frederic buys a pistol formerly owned by "an officer who was an excellent shot" but not excellent enough to avoid being killed.

In a hotel room for their last hours, Catherine looks at the room's gaudy embellishments—red plush curtains, a chandelier, and too many mirrors—and confesses to feeling "like a whore." She responds uncannily to Frederic's unspoken annoyance with her discomfort by instantly ridding herself of it; the edge gone from her voice, she visibly calms down and reassures him that "[she is] a good girl again" (159). Some questions are raised here. Is this exchange of words and feelings at this moment believable? Has Catherine separated herself from her emotions to save this union or perhaps just the evening? Has her love become genuinely selfless? Or did she simply remember that these trappings of crass promiscuity have nothing to do with her and their private world of meaning? Why, also, was

Frederic annoyed? Perhaps this is Hemingway's lapse: not noticing what his words might be suggesting. In the end, they make a home for themselves in the garish room, as they always attempt to do, wherever they are.

"Have you got a father?" asks Frederic when Catherine offhandedly mentions that alcohol caused her father to develop gout. With this reference to a father comes the first sense of the past, of either of them having a personal history or of belonging to other people. With this intrusive reference to the past comes the awareness of time that has been largely missing in their romantic affair; it has been taking place in a suspension of time. Hemingway has his narrator quote from one of the literature's best-known utterances about time, Andrew Marvell's seventeenth-century poem, "To His Coy Mistress," the first line of which—"Had we but world enough, or time"—inspired one of many potential titles he considered for his novel.

Marvell's poem is doubly apt here. The poet knows that even an age's worth of time is insufficient to recount every last one of his love's charms, but "at [his] back [he] always hears / Time's winged chariot hurrying near"; and so he urges her to let go of "coyness" and permit passion and his seduction to triumph. Although Frederic's twentieth-century seduction needs less persuading to be successful than a seventeenth-century seduction might have required, this particular awareness of time is new for him; the pervasive death in wartime has forced him to see the transient nature of love, as has the nature of the love itself. For Catherine, the poem has meaning as well, although she euphemistically states (or deliberately misstates) that the poem is "about a girl who wouldn't live with a man" when it is actually the speaker's explicit and quite urgent plea to his lover to "sport us while we may. . . . And tear our pleasures with rough strife / through the iron gates of life." This was the gesture she withheld from her fiancé; her regret for this "error" is never far from her mind.

In the concluding pages of Book Two, the word "time" appears four times. As they leave for the train station and Frederic's departure, Catherine wishes, as she once did in vain, that her love came back to her quickly with "just a little [wound] in the foot" (162).

In Chapter XXIV, Catherine and Frederic perform the iconic lovers' separation, in this case, in the rain. Also iconic is the scene of a train crowded with soldiers headed to the front. Once again, Frederic acknowledges a lapse of judgment—paying someone to hold a seat while he is off with Catherine—that suggests an unseemly selfishness. He recognizes the lapse and gives his seat to a soldier who has been waiting for two hours.

Book Three

Chapter XXV returns the narrative to the scenes and actions of war. "It did not feel like a homecoming," thinks Frederic. The cold, wet weather of fall has set in, and Frederic hears bad news about the war effort repeated many times by the major. War weariness has also set in, and no one thinks the Americans will arrive to help at the Italian front. Rinaldi's comradely teasing about guarding Frederic's glass, until he returned to his old way of "brushing away harlotry with a toothbrush," reminds the reader that Frederic is a changed man, no longer likely to visit the brothels. He also resists Rinaldi's adolescent and disrespectful notion that women are valuable only for the sexual favors they perform for men. Frederic misses Catherine, but being back in Rinaldi's ribald and affectionate company is some compensation. Anyone who calls himself "the snake of reason," as Rinaldi does, is providing an entertaining distraction from the war.

The priest arrives for dinner, making a foursome with the major. The good-natured banter turns uncomfortably unpleasant when Rinaldi notices that Frederic moves to quell the priest baiting that used to dominate the mealtimes. Feeling isolated, Rinaldi astutely observes a change in Frederic, which he interprets as a shift in Frederic's loyalties: "There he is, gone over with the priest." As Rinaldi turns confrontational, the priest calms the scene with his gentle, forgiving spirit and suggests that the overworked doctor deserves a leave. As the men leave, the major makes explicit what Rinaldi's outbursts have suggested—that the doctor is worried he has syphilis and is treating himself with Salvarsan (the standard treatment at the time).

Some readers have expressed confusion about Rinaldi's lavish expressions of affection for Frederic. One of Hemingway's early critics, Clifton P. Fadiman, believed Hemingway was unaware of the two conclusions readers might come to—the homosexual and/or sentimental—and argued that the author was intent on "[making] us feel that this very sense of comradeship—nordically reticent in [Frederic] Henry's case, blasphemously, ironically effusive in Rinaldi's—was one of the few things that mitigated the horror and stupidity of the war" (Fadiman, "A Fine American Novel," *Critical Essays on Hemingway's 'A Farewell to Arms,'* ed. George Monteiro 82).

In Chapter XXVI, Frederic discusses the war's development with the priest who reports that conditions have grown worse, with morale lower than ever. Frederic briefly initiates a conversation that looks for understanding within religious, mainly Christian language. This is new for him—revealing a deepening respect for the priest and his presence among the men and possibly revealing a deepening sense of war as an adversary of love. Whatever the explanation, it is clear he has been thinking all this time without being quite deliberate about it: "I never think and yet when I begin to talk I say the thing I have found out in my mind without thinking" (185).

In the brief discussion about what each side will do to end the war, Hemingway introduces speculation about the power of defeat to generate wisdom and the power of power to generate greater and more corrupt power, but he leaves the notion undeveloped.

There are more visual reminders in Chapter XXVII of the physical damage war inflicts on villages and the vulnerable countryside. There is also more evidence of the extensive research Hemingway undertook to understand the details of geography and military strategy that he would not have known from personal experience. Praise for the accuracy of Hemingway's details and his realistic portrayal of the Italian participation in the war was, and still is, widespread.

Frederic has arrived at the front at Bainsizza to receive his new assignments. With his contact, Gino, he discusses military strategy that so far in the novel he has not shown any way of having acquired except for the random newspaper reports he read during the Milan stay. Clearly, however, he has been thinking extensively. The tactical questions he asks frequently receive inadequate answers, a sure sign of the weariness and subsequent ill-preparedness of the Italian forces. The surrounding landscape of broken houses and rutted roads and the weather patterns of alternating snow and cold rain that make for mud and standing water everywhere add to the prevailing sense of doom.

Some effort is made to undo the rumors of retreat, but, in the end, it is plain that retreat is unavoidable. German forces are rumored to have joined the Austrians, and "the word 'Germans' was something to be frightened of" (193). The retreat begins in language reminiscent of that in Chapter I—just as dark and hopeless, but not as distant. The reader now has a more developed familiarity with some of the soldiers, which renders their individual fates more palpable and lamentable:

> The retreat was orderly, wet and sullen. In the night, going slowly along the crowded roads we passed troops marching under the rain, guns, horses pulling wagons, mules, motor trucks, all moving away from the front. . . . [In] Gorizia . . . we came up the street [where] they were loading the girls from the soldiers' whorehouse into a truck. There were seven girls. . . . Two of them were crying.

Add to this scene the apparent indifference of nature toward the fate of these men and women in retreat and toward that of the bystanders in their wrecked villages, as well as the shivering pack animals, and a bleaker picture of the realm of the living would be hard to imagine.

Before the retreat, Frederic has an important conversation about patriotism that is essential for understanding Hemingway's perspective in the novel. For Gino, patriotism is ardent and dutiful service to his country, but he is no fanatic; he calls the soil of the Bainsizza "sacred," but he is also pragmatic: he "[wishes] it grew more potatoes" (190). At the same time, he cannot even bear to think that the terrible and costly fighting he has witnessed all summer could be "in vain." In contrast, Frederic feels a need to withdraw from the conversation, confessing to the reader that words like "sacred," "glorious," "sacrifice," and "in vain" have caused him "embarrassment." He reflects on the possible explanations for his response:

> We had heard [these words], sometimes standing in the rain almost out of earshot, so that only the shouted words came through, and had read them, on proclamations that were slapped up by billposters over other proclamations, now for a long time, and I had seen nothing sacred, and the things that were glorious had no glory and the sacrifices were like the stockyards of Chicago. . . . There were many words that you could not stand to hear and finally only the names of places had dignity. . . . Abstract words such as glory, honor, courage, or hallow were obscene beside the concrete names of villages, the numbers of roads, the names of rivers, the numbers of regiments and the dates. (191)

This attitude is definitive of the postwar period in American history and was manifested in different ways by members of the lost generation of which Hemingway was a part. It represents the terrible disillusionment that followed the savage and meaningless carnage of World War I, when all values were emptied of meaning and nothing of value was perceived as sustainable or incorruptible. Referring to Frederic's dismissal of these words, Hemingway scholar Thomas Strychacz recalls the assault on clichéd language made by writers contemporary with Hemingway, specifically James Joyce and Ezra Pound. T.S. Eliot was another, writing with scorn and despair about the tyranny of cliché in "The Love Song of J. Alfred Prufrock" and *The Waste Land.*
  Strychacz writes:

Recognizing cliché is a mode of understanding, and expressing, mechanical lifestyles, routinized psyches, formulaic mass cultures, and worn-out aesthetics—characteristics that are held to identify Anglo-American culture (Pound), Ireland (Joyce), and Spain (Hemingway), but more generally the conditions of modernity in the West. (*Dangerous Masculinities*, 2008: 54)

As the column of trucks wends its way haltingly through the rainy woods in Chapter XXVIII, Frederic discovers that his crew has taken four stragglers aboard—two sergeants and two young girls. The girls speak a dialect no one understands, and their behavior makes clear they are terrified to be alone in the company of men. Aymo tries to have what he thinks of as a little harmless fun with them, but they flinch in terror at the slightest gesture, and he finally stops. Blank spaces on the page substitute for many of the words that frighten the girls and offended the Boston censors. Where did these girls come from? They form an archetypal image of innocence and extreme vulnerability. Frederic seems to have noticed this quality when he describes them as a pair of wild birds. Their unexplained appearance in the dark and menacing woods calls to mind all the innocent bystanders whose lives are thrown into turmoil by war.

Frederic drifts into sleep thinking about the girls and begins to dream about Catherine. The dream seems to give a different kind of expression to much of the substance of the novel. Frederic's vision of Catherine has moved from erotic to maternal, and he assumes a caretaking role, thinking about how to make her comfortable. There is a tenderness and reverence fitting to thoughts of love and the new life they are creating, but these feelings are disturbingly mixed with ones suggesting death in a bed with white sheets. In addition, everything is happening in the rain. It is a dream both comforting and disturbing.

Frederic makes a critical judgment when he chooses a different route for the retreat of his own convoy. Two small gestures described in this scene illustrate the way that decorum and respect can survive in the midst of the inhumanity of war. At the deserted farmhouse where they briefly stop for food, Frederic orders one of the men to put back a clock he is trying to steal; and another man leaves the wine jug just inside the shut-up house so "[the] Austrians can find it without breaking down the door" (209).

Shooting a deserter was a controversial practice. In Chapter XXIX, Frederic shoots and wounds—and Bonello kills—one of the sergeants on the run after disobeying Frederic's order to gather brush to get the truck unstuck. It happens suddenly, without warning, and it is shocking to many readers and critics. For one thing, Hemingway introduces the possibility for reader disapproval when he has the sergeants state with conviction that technically they cannot be commanded to do anything by an American ambulance driver. Again, why would Frederic as the narrator of his own story include this description of such an impulsive and consequential act? Especially puzzling is the juxtaposition of the kind consideration Frederic and Bonello have just extended to the sergeants with the merciless killing of one of them. In an essay contributed to *Hemingway's Italy*, Linda Wagner-Martin writes:

> Hemingway's style intensifies the impersonality of this killing. Bonello's bragging, Frederic's demand for authority, . . . the sense that killing was what a person had to do in wartime all jar against the humane treatment these same men had given the young Italian sisters. The word choice "dropped one" also places the killing into the realm of sport shooting. ("At the Heart of *A Farewell to Arms*," *Hemingway's Italy* 164)

Frederic's judgment about taking a different road was both a mistake and a blessing: they are forced to make their flight on foot after abandoning their vehicles in the mud, but Frederic hears the sounds of firing indicating that, as he had expected, Austrian planes were attacking the Italian forces retreating on the regular route. As they walk toward Udine ("going fast against time"), Frederic listens to the others talk jovially about socialism.

In Chapter XXX, the menacing presence of war closes in on Frederic and the others as they make their way through the ravaged landscape. The sudden sighting of the contingent of German soldiers on the road above is a shock to them and to the reader. The Germans are robust and confident; the retreating soldiers and civilians are weary and demoralized. As they come upon two bridges—one blown up, the other left intact—they are baffled by whatever strategy is responsible for this kind of randomness. Moments later, they encounter a different kind of randomness when a single shot of friendly fire from "spooked-out" members of the Italian rear guard kills Aymo. Piani, Bonello, and Frederic leave the scene. As Frederic looks back at Aymo's body left on the muddy embankment, a cap placed reverently over his face, he thinks: "I had liked him as well as any one I ever knew" (222).

An abandoned farmhouse provides temporary refuge and better-than-nothing nourishment for a few brief hours; it is especially sheltering for Frederic because in the hay mow he falls into a pleasant reverie about playing in a barn as a child. With all the war's turbulence, anguish, and anxiety relegated to a distance, for this brief interlude, Frederic can feel a measure of safety and think, "The hay smelled good and lying in a barn in the hay took away all the years in between" (224). Moments later Piani reluctantly divulges that Bonello has run off, declaring more willingness to be a prisoner than to be shot. Technically this makes Bonello a deserter and disobedient to authority, but Frederic decides to spare his family by not reporting his disappearance as a desertion. One wonders, however, if either man, as each was making his separate and pivotal decision, remembered how hours earlier they had treated the disobedient sergeant for a similar offense. Frederic's thoughts here are an important preface to a life-changing decision he will soon face.

Finally, wet, exhausted, and in pain from all the walking, they join the line of retreat, and Frederic has another revelation about the absurdity of war: "We had walked through two armies without incident. . . . No one had bothered us when we were in plain sight along the roadway. The killing came suddenly and unreasonably" (226). They make their way safely over a bridge hanging perilously close to the raging water beneath. Anticipating respite and security once they get to the other side, they encounter instead the most threatening and inexplicable spectacle of the war so far: the Italian battle police lining up and questioning the officers who, in the chaos of the retreat, had become separated from their men and then, one by one, summarily shooting them for desertion. Assumed to be a spy or a traitor because he is heard speaking Italian with an accent, Frederic is held against his will and thrust into the line of doomed officers being questioned.

Hemingway keenly felt the insanity of war, and in this scene he seems intent on exposing a stark example of it: beleaguered patriots accused without evidence of treason for events beyond their control by fellow officers, who, when presented with extenuating descriptions of the chaotic retreat, respond dismissively with high-minded but empty rhetoric about how "Italy should never retreat." While deciding whether to attempt an escape or allow himself to be questioned, Frederic thinks:

> I saw how their minds worked; if they had minds and if they worked. They were all young men and they were saving their country. . . . The questioners had that beautiful detachment and devotion to stern justice of men dealing in death without being in any danger of it. (233)

Seeing a chance for escape, Frederic dives into the fast-flowing river he has just safely crossed; when he surfaces, the shoreline with its battle police and doomed officers has passed out of sight. Now he, too, with the anonymous sergeant and Bonello, has become a deserter.

Desertion is an inflammatory subject, and nearly every commentator on the novel has something to say about it. Many make the obvious point that Frederic's desertion is an act of cowardice, particularly unbecoming because he had taken no time to reflect before shooting at the deserting sergeant. Others quickly make the other obvious point that the hotheaded battle police are sparing no one and will almost certainly execute Frederic within minutes. One of the more thoughtful commentaries appears in *Teaching Hemingway's "A Farewell to Arms"* in the essay by two military officers who teach the novel at the U.S. Air Force Academy (see Niday and Meredith's contribution, pp. 113–131).

An example of another thoughtful commentary is that of Kim Moreland, who, writing in *The Medievalist Impulse in American Literature: Twain, Adams, Fitzgerald, and Hemingway*, points out that:

> The modern army is often presented as a large, inefficient bureaucracy where important information cannot make it through channels and important orders are given too late. Confusion thus reigns in the huge retreat of the Italian army. . . . Frederic Henry is disgusted by the complete lack of order and discipline that results in the senseless execution of the Italian officers by other Italian officers—a breakdown in leadership [that was historically accurate about the retreat from Caporetto]. Frederic deserts from the army at this point, making his "separate peace" (*FA* 243). Yet he deserts not from a general horror of war as such, as this action is often interpreted, but because his army is led by men who in turning on their fellows betray the chivalric values of loyalty and comradeship. (169)

In an earlier chapter when Frederic and his men have just spotted the Germans and their hopes for a safe passage to Udine are waning, Frederic feels a spasm of panic and then quickly brings himself back to his senses: "The thing to do was to be calm and not get shot at or captured" (219). In Chapter XXXI, he must again summon this presence of mind—a quality Hemingway famously called "grace under pressure." Powerful forces of nature—in this case flood-level water coursing down the river—are indifferent to Frederic's fate, and he must gather all his courage, experience, intelligence, fortitude, and physical strength to stay aware and keep abreast of the current and steer himself toward the shore. After making it out of the water, he must then survive the wet and cold weather and his disorientation and disconnection from time and place. He remembers to cut off the identifying stars from his sleeves and to secure them with his money in an inside pocket. Finally reaching a road, he disguises his identity by lowering his head and limping when he passes troops going in the other direction.

Hemingway's own experience and the research he undertook to understand what he did not know personally are again evident in this chapter when Frederic describes in an almost reverent tone details of the routes he takes and the elements of the landscape he traverses. He reaches a rail line, and, like that other American adventurer, Huck Finn on his raft, Frederic hops a freight train, outsmarts the guards, finds a hiding place under the canvas protecting a shipment of guns, and heads out, his destination certain, a safe arrival not.

In a state of mind that suggests the condition once referred to as shell shock and now called post-traumatic stress disorder (PTSD), Frederic reflects in Chapter XXXII on fragments of his war experience. In critic Michael Reynolds's essay "*A Farewell to Arms:* Doctors in the House of Love," this issue is discussed at length. Reynolds points out a number of changes Frederic exhibits after his violent wounding: his difficulty sleeping at night, his confusion about night and day, his confession to Count Greffi that religious feeling is only present for him at night, his change in attitude toward the priest, and the transformation in his relationship with Catherine from "a game" to an unintended but compelling and irresistible love. "Like a victim of shell shock," Reynolds writes, "[Frederic] exhibits altered feelings, affection, temper, and habits" (*The Cambridge Companion to Hemingway*, 1996, 120). Catherine, too, appears to be a victim, although not of a physical wounding. Remorse and a broken heart have made her "crazy."

Frederic's altered state is only made worse by another trauma: the frightful encounter with the battle police, the daring suddenness of his escape, and his prolonged exposure to cold and perilous water. The combined effect has brought about a change in perspective that brings him to an important insight: "Anger [had been] washed away in the river along with any obligation" (241). Everything passes before him in equal measure now—Catherine (whom he has enough presence of mind to know not to think about too much), Rinaldi, syphilis, guns, Piani, his knee, leaky canvas and vaselined metal, his uniform and stars, his identifying papers, and how his disappearance would be recorded. Only his overriding hunger, which he turns into an abstraction, disconnected from the rest of himself—"[My belly] was very hungry in there. I could feel it turn over on itself" (240)—dominates his wandering thoughts.

Book Four

Frederic's disguise fails the first time it is tested, but no harm ensues. A wine shop/café proprietor noticed Frederic when he jumped off the decelerating train, and later, after Frederic comes in for some coffee and bread, the proprietor notices the space on the coat where the stars have been ripped off and advises him to get rid of it. The wine shop seems to be functioning as a safe haven; Frederic is offered shelter and assured that he will not be reported, but, after taking note of the offer, he heads off in search of Catherine. At the hospital, he finds the porter and his wife; when they ask after him, he answers "Fine"—precisely the understated and uncomplaining response Hemingway's code of honor expected of his heroes. The kindness of the proprietor and the solicitude Frederic receives from these two former acquaintances are clearly intentional on the author's part; the wrongheaded battle police are not the only representation of the Italian character.

Throughout Chapter XXXIII, a noteworthy change occurs: Frederic's life has moved from peril, deprivation, and menacing obstructions to offers of shelter and protection, ease, generosity, and food. His old acquaintance, the singing student Simmons, is relieved to see him safely away from the front, asks for no explanations, and offers him a set of his own clothes ("all the clothes you want") to aid Frederic's disguise. The plan is to go first to Stresa where Catherine and Ferguson have gone and then to Switzerland for a respite with Catherine. Life may be moving more easily for Frederic now, but it is still abundantly dramatic; he must stay in disguise and row a boat across Lake Maggiore to escape the Italian police.

Another Hemingway critic, John Robert Bittner, makes a point relevant to this section of the narrative when he calls attention to what he perceives as the anti-Fascist elements in the novel. *A Farewell to Arms* was banned in Italy by Mussolini until after World War II. Mussolini had been at the same front as Frederic had been and was personally familiar with the catastrophic Italian retreat from Caporetto. It is also well known that Hemingway was contemptuous of Mussolini and the ideas behind fascism. Bittner writes:

> In addition to the novel's emphasis on the Caporetto retreat, the subtexts in *A Farewell to Arms* were guilty of befouling two of Fascism's most important symbols: a military uniform and the glory of Rome. . . . In [the novel] Hemingway makes a point of interweaving the symbolism of Frederic's uniform into the narrative. When Frederic discards his military uniform, even though a uniform of 1917, he discards an important symbol of postwar Fascist Italy. [In the train he] thinks to himself: "I would have liked to have had the uniform off. . . . I had taken off the stars. . . . [it] was no point of honor" (*FTA* 232). (Bittner, "Anti-Fascist Symbols and Subtexts in *A Farewell to Arms*," *Hemingway's Italy* 103–104)

In this chapter, Hemingway also injects some negative reflections about Rome into Simmons's conversation with Frederic. When Frederic asks his friend for civilian clothes because he has left his in Rome, back when he had had an interest in architecture, Simmons calls Rome "a filthy place" and scorns its architecture. In an earlier chapter, Frederic, Rinaldi, and the mayor engage in some lighthearted banter disdainful of Rome: "'[Rome] is hot and full of fleas. . . . Rome is the mother of nations. It will never forget Romulus suckling the Tiber . . .'" (76). Bittner writes:

Even more important than the Fascist uniform was the myth of the Roman Empire, invoked so often to instill Italian patriotism that it took on the qualities of a religion. . . . [In the passage quoted above] Frederic is not really scorning Rome. This is the banter of friends who have been drinking, friends who need release from the tension of the front. . . . [The] real target behind the banter is the ultra patriotic rhetoric, always implicit, upon which Mussolini and his henchmen depended. For the totalitarian mind, the banter of a Rinaldi and a Frederic Henry would be unacceptable. (104–105)

Frederic experiences another transformation as he abandons his uniform and replaces it with civilian clothes. "I missed the feeling of being held by your own clothes," he thinks (252). But, in Chapter XXXIV, he is determinedly on his way toward a different life, one suddenly possible by his having made what he famously calls his "separate peace" with the war. The change proves to be real when he discovers on the train bound to Stresa from Milan that he is not unduly bothered by the scornful gazes directed at him by men his age in their aviator uniforms. Abstract words like "glory," "honor," and "patriotism" no longer have the power to embarrass him. However, just moments after the aviators get off the train, leaving Frederic to his own thoughts he realizes, " . . . I did not have the feeling that it was really over. I had the feeling of a boy who thinks of what is happening at a certain hour at the schoolhouse from which he has played truant" (254).

Reunited with Catherine and Fergy in a hotel dining room, Frederic must endure a bittersweet and sometimes comical tirade from Fergy who accuses him of being a disgraceful "snake with an Italian uniform"; once again it seems obvious that Fergy's loneliness and possible memory of an earlier love fuel her dislike of Frederic and her dismay over Catherine's pregnancy and imminent departure with him. The mix of repressed longing, anger, and fear of loneliness in Fergy is almost palpable. Frederic is understandably annoyed by her remarks, but Fergy acknowledges her own unreasonableness.

Frederic and Catherine spend the night in the hotel and awake to the morning sun streaming through the window. During the night, Frederic falls into intermittent reveries— mainly about the bliss of awakening to find that Catherine and not the war is his reality now. But he also considers the darker realities that reflect, even more than war weariness, a general defeat of hope and a presaging of Catherine's fate. He thinks:

> If people bring so much courage to this world the world has to kill them to break them, so of course it kills them. The world breaks every one and afterward many are strong at the broken places. But those that will not break it kills. It kills the very good and the very gentle and the very brave impartially. If you are none of these you can be sure that it will kill you too but there will be no special hurry. (258–259)

This passage is among the most quotable of Hemingway's writings. The author's observation has both poetry and truth, but since there are many notably brave people who live long lives devoted to justice and compassion, it cannot be said to be universally true. These are rather more the thoughtful reflections of one who has witnessed a part of history in which human beings have—with particular brutality and senselessness—transgressed against one another. The American ambulance driver at the beginning of the novel who thinks the war "has nothing to do with [him]" is not the same man who is here trying to make sense of senseless events. The words express eloquently a kind of spiritual death.

The chapter ends with Frederic and Catherine shutting out the rest of the world as they draw closer to each other. There are two worlds: love and war; home and not home; criminal and not criminal; Italy and Switzerland.

Although Frederic knows the danger of being seen in public, he chooses to leave his hotel room in Chapter XXXV ostensibly to join the barman in an hour of fishing on the lake but more likely to check out the logistics of the clandestine escape by boat he knows may be necessary to get him and Catherine safely to Switzerland. Through the sympathetic barman, he secures the use of the boat key: his passage to freedom once again unobstructed in contrast to his passage through the mountains with the caravan of ambulances.

Many readers and critics of *A Farewell to Arms* comment on the nature of the romantic love that unites Catherine and Frederic, some even noticing the seeds of its failure in the words each uses to describe the relationship. The brief conversation that occurs in the hotel bedroom after Frederic returns from fishing is a good illustration of these concerns.

Catherine begins:

> "What's the matter, darling?"
> "I don't know."
> "I know. You haven't anything to do. All you have is me and I go away."
> "That's true."
> "I'm sorry, darling. I know it must be a dreadful feeling to have nothing at all suddenly."
> "My life used to be full of everything," I said. "Now if you aren't with me I haven't a thing in the world." (266)

The notion that lovers are nothing without each other has many illustrations in literature, notably in Catherine Earnshaw's defiant declaration in *Wuthering Heights*: "I am Heathcliff." There are many instances in Hemingway's novel when Catherine, in particular, is so completely devoted to serving Frederic's needs that she goes beyond the line from selfless giving (which is always admirable) to self-effacement (which hints at self-destruction). When, in Chapter XVIII, Catherine is explaining why she does not need the formality of a marriage certificate, she tells Frederic, "There isn't any me. I'm you. Don't make up a separate me" (119). These feelings become explicitly religious a moment later when she tells Frederic, "You're my religion. You're all I've got" (120). Writing about these issues, critic Mark Spilka observes that this declaration is:

a time-honored Christian Romantic version of the union of two souls. . . . But Catherine and (more ambivalently) Frederic are Romantics whose Christianity has lapsed . . . and so invokes a Romantic heresy, the religion of love, going back to the eleventh century. . . . Lacking any connection with God or immortality, this atheistic faith will eventually fail them, leaving the ambivalent Frederic alone and bereft with the memories here recalled. But for a time they are fused in mystic selflessness. (*Hemingway's Quarrel with Androgyny*, 1990, 214)

In the dining room with Catherine and Ferguson, Frederic meets up with Count Greffi, a literate and cultured European gentleman of such an advanced age that Frederic tells the reader that the count's niece, who has accompanied him, reminds him of his own grandmother. Later, Frederic plays a game of billiards with the count. Dismissing any notion of possessing the wisdom of old age, the count steers the conversation toward matters of love and religion, subjects about which his wisdom is very much in evidence. He is wise in knowing that nothing is certain, wise also in knowing that he cannot feign a feeling of devoutness, which he greatly laments not having. The two play their game together—playfully and respectfully challenging each other, sipping wine between shots, speaking alternately in English and Italian. It is the most civilized scene in the novel: a reminder of what life can be without war.

As the two part company, the count says to Frederic, "I hope you will be very fortunate, very happy, and very, very healthy" (272). In a matter of months, Frederic will be both unfortunate and unhappy—his own best-laid plans and the wishes of the count notwithstanding.

In Chapter XXXVI, like a harbinger of the ill to come, the nighttime rain blows through the open hotel window and awakens Frederic just as the barman's knock comes to announce the alarming news of Frederic's imminent arrest. The generosity of Emilio the bartender is not met in Frederic's promised gift of pipe tobacco, because Frederic "just missed" having provided it, but it is another instance of the Italian goodwill that Hemingway is eager to illustrate. In a rare moment of irony, Catherine remarks as they begin their escape from the hotel into a cold and windy November rain, "It's a lovely night for a walk" (276). The startled porter sends them off with an umbrella and, when they reach the boat, they learn that Emilio has stocked it with food and spirits. The generosity of both porter and barman is genuine, but Frederic insists on paying something for these life-saving gifts; as they head off into the dark and the storm with a destination but no certainty of safely arriving there, the scene recalls the plight of the virginal sisters who also needed rescue and escape and had only Frederic's 10-lira note to aid their search for refuge.

The ordeal of rowing in the dark across the cold and white-capped lake from Italy to Switzerland—a distance of 35 kilometers (almost 22 miles)—is described in Chapter XXXVII, but aside from questions about navigation and a brief mention of his blistered hands, Frederic remains stoic and determined. Catherine, as well, refrains from calling attention to what was surely an arduous and frightful time for her. It is not clear which dénouement would be worse—the possibility of capsizing and drowning or being spotted by customs officials or guards from either side—but neither happens. When the umbrella that has been rigged as a sail suddenly inverts on Frederic, Catherine is able to laugh, transforming a moment of failed navigation into a comical adventure. Love, perhaps, and/or adrenalin makes for high spirits, and the playful spirit they maintain with each other throughout the long night is admirable and endearing. Landing safely in a Swiss village makes them giddy; the rain, the ground of a new country under their feet, the prospect of rolls for breakfast—they cannot believe their good fortune. Their "cockeyed excitement" turns into amused detachment as they are peremptorily arrested and sent on their way. Their money, manners, and worldly experience ease the beginning and the end of this voyage for them, but not the middle passage which is all courage, love, and good nature.

Book Five

An interlude of bliss follows in Chapter XXXVIII. Frederic and Catherine are lodged in an idyllic spot in the Swiss countryside outside the town of Montreux where they can see the lake and the mountains beyond from their room and breakfast is brought to them by cheerful Mrs. Guttingen. Hemingway's descriptive details of the chalet, their rented room, their simple daily routine of eating, hiking, playing cards, reading, eating again, and sleeping are as evocative as those in the beginning pages of the novel, but to entirely different effect. Their life during these months is edenic; Frederic thinks, "The war seemed as far away as the football games of someone else's college" (301).

Brief forays into the village bring them in contact with the larger world. Frederic buys newspapers that communicate a single message: "Everything was going badly everywhere" (302), but not with Frederic and Catherine. This is their time to wander, dream, explore, and make plans. They discuss marriage again, but Catherine, in a minor display of vanity she has not exposed before, is firmly against marrying until she is thin again and all the guests can think, "what a handsome young couple" (304). Later, she shows a different aspect of herself—an uneasiness or anxiety that Frederic may grow tired of her in her "matronly state." Frederic's reassurances seem genuine, but when he takes up her suggestion to grow a beard, he seems pleased that "[it] will give [him] something to do" (308).

These odd, but fleeting moments hint at the ultimate insufficiency of one person to satisfy all the needs of the other, the fatal flaw of romantic love, but the drama of their situation and Catherine's pregnancy keep the pair engaged and mutually devoted. There are, however, two moments where the ideal of romantic union moves embarrassingly close to absurdity. The first occurs when Catherine is so keen on becoming one with Frederic that she wishes she had been afflicted with a bout of the same gonorrhea he had suffered earlier in his life "to be like [him]" (309). The second incident occurs when, awake in the night at the same time, Catherine insists they fall back asleep at the same instant. It does not happen, of course, and it is unrealistic or overly romanticized thinking to believe that it could. The discussion about Catherine's having her hair cut short and Frederic's letting his hair grow long is another illustration of the same delusion. They decide to play a game of chess, which, with its required concentration on something other than the self, comes as a relief.

The brief Chapter XXXIX concludes their idyll. Frederic has grown his beard, and several snowstorms have left the ground hard packed, so that, for Catherine, getting about requires wearing hobnailed boots and carrying a sharp steel-pointed stick. Their world seems almost make-believe in this portion of the novel. They drink a spicy wine with earring-wearing chamois hunters and have fantasies about being foxes with tails to wrap around themselves at night. The thought of the lives of others is intrusive: Frederic does not want to think about his first family, which "quarreled so much it wore itself out," and he worries that the first member of their second family—the couple's not-yet-born child whom he calls "a little brat"—will come between them, and she vows not to let that happen.

The idyll ends with this ambiguous and premonitory exchange about what life will be like after "young Catherine" is born:

> ". . . and maybe [I'll] look lovely, darling, and be so thin and exciting to you that you'll fall in love with me all over again."
>
> "Hell. I love you enough now. What do you want to do? Ruin me?"
>
> "Yes. I want to ruin you."
>
> "Good. That's what I want too." (315)

Spring rains and snowmelt turn the mountaintop paradise to slush and mud. In the next-to-last chapter, Frederic and Catherine leave the home they have made for themselves and depart for Lausanne where the hospital is, but not before arranging with their hosts to return later in the spring with "the little one." It is raining when they take a room in the hotel in town. While Catherine tries to arrange the space to make it feel more homelike, Frederic reads the papers and makes note of the date: "It was March, 1918, and the German offensive had started in France" (318). This observation feels like an intrusion into their private world of collective bliss and time. It is the first mention of a real date in historical time with events unrelated to their personal lives. The timeless quality of their mountaintop life begins to dissipate and recede in Chapter XL, and the conditions of space and the temporal world—the human condition—begin to close in on them again. To the extent that they are able, Catherine and Frederic duplicate their mountaintop life in the city, taking walks and finding interesting places to eat. Catherine buys baby clothes, and Frederic visits the gymnasium for exercise. Although they understand it differently than it will turn out, these are their last moments alone together, and they know it. Frederic writes:

We knew the baby was very close now and it gave us both a feeling as though something were hurrying us and we could not lose any time together. (321)

Catherine's labor begins in Chapter XLI. In the hospital, she lists "none" as her religion and is taken to her room. Her labor is protracted, and the pain of the contractions increases. Characteristically, Catherine does not complain about the pain, but inexplicably she seems to have a need to apologize for having a long labor and causing inconvenience to the doctor. Her apologetic tone has been much commented on, some finding her, as before, absurdly self-effacing, taking on a burden of guilt women have been socialized to bear; others find her selflessness genuine and admirable.

Most of the chapter centers on the inaction of waiting for something to happen. Frederic is alternately banished and summoned from and to the hospital. Waiting finally leads to a delirium of worry: what if she dies? A decision is made to perform a cesarian. On the way to the operating room, Frederic notices two nurses racing to the room with excitement at the prospect of observing the procedure. To them, the event is an opportunity to increase their medical knowledge. To Frederic, it is a matter of life and death. To Catherine, it means the relief of intractable pain. To the attending doctors, the birth is a professional challenge. As it turns out, the focus of all the attention, the unborn son, is already dead in its mother's womb; for him, the procedure is too late.

Frederic, in a frenzy of waiting, pictures life as a cruel game:

> That was what you did. You died. You did not know what it was about. You never had time to learn. They threw you in and told you the rules and the first time they caught you off base they killed you. (338)

Then he recalls a moment from his youth when he had a chance to save some ants from dying. The ants were trapped on a log that had been thrown onto a fire. Each strategy for survival was doomed; the only difference was the timing and manner of each ant's demise. Frederic briefly considered his chance to act as the ants' savior but chose not to act, or to act, but in his own self-interest. He emptied his tin cup of water onto the log so that he could refill it with whisky. The steam produced by the dousing clearly did not save the ants but possibly prolonged their deaths. This passage encapsulates the stark view of life associated with naturalism and modernism. It bitterly illustrates the futility of effort or intervention in the face of forces too huge to alter or control. The hopes for the future that Frederic and Catherine hold, that all people hold, the good intentions and the efforts—all these are useless against the flow of natural forces.

Frederic prays for Catherine to live, but she dies. The priest prays for the war to end, but it does not. Human beings are born with hopes and dreams inherent to their nature, but there is no one and no thing in the universe that responds to, recognizes, or fulfills them. Hemingway has made this bleak view of human life repeatedly in *A Farewell to Arms*, in the words that come in Frederic's reflections and in the unfolding series of actions that end with Catherine's and their son's deaths. Frederic is not even able to make his separate peace with Catherine at the end; with the life gone from her body, saying farewell is "like saying goodbye to a statue" (343).

Frederic has to tell his story for the reason all stories of love and loss are told—to share them with others so that the individual will not have to bear the pain alone. But what did Frederic mean at the beginning of his story, when he told the reader that the priest knew something then that he would later learn? Whether attending to the unceasing flow of heartrending war casualties or putting up with the soldiers' relentless teasing about his celibacy, the priest has about him an unshakable equanimity as well as happiness that comes from loving God which, as the priest makes explicit, means having a wish to serve others, a wish to sacrifice. Death, Catherine tells Frederic as she is dying, is "just a dirty trick." The priest tells Frederic that, in his beloved home country, he is spared the teasing because there "it is understood [that loving God as the priest does] is not a dirty joke." But the priest is not living in the place that makes him comfortable; he is serving where he is perhaps least at home.

There are others in the novel who serve. Rinaldi is devoted to saving lives, Piani chooses to stay with Frederic rather than to desert, Gino happily serves his country. Catherine serves as well. Even in dying, she still ministers to Frederic, reassuring him that her love is undying but also that he will find love elsewhere after she is gone. She dies with dignity, bearing the pain of childbirth without complaint, good natured and generous as she has been throughout. Loving Frederic has saved her from bitterness.

Hemingway leaves the reader with no clear sense of what will become of Frederic. At the end, he can only repeat to those who try to comfort him that there is nothing to do and nothing to say. Frederic is not Catherine, and he is not the priest, but it seems likely that he is thinking of what both their lives have meant as he walks back to his hotel in the rain.

Critical Views

CARLOS BAKER ON *A FAREWELL TO ARMS* AS HEMINGWAY'S *ROMEO AND JULIET*

The position occupied by *A Farewell to Arms* among Hemingway's tragic writings may be suggested by the fact that he once referred to the story of Lieutenant Frederic Henry and Catherine Barkley as his *Romeo and Juliet*.[4] The most obvious parallel is that Henry and Catherine, like their Elizabethan prototypes, might be seen as star-crossed lovers. Hemingway might also have been thinking of how rapidly Romeo and Juliet, whose affair has begun as a mere flirtation, pass over into the status of relatively mature lovers. In the third place, he may have meant to imply that his own lovers, caught in the tragic pattern of the war on the Austrian–Italian front, are not far different from the young victims of the Montague-Capulet family feud.

Neither in *Romeo and Juliet* nor in *A Farewell to Arms* is the catastrophe a direct and logical result of the immoral social situation. Catherine's bodily structure, which precludes a normal delivery for her baby, is an unfortunate biological accident. The death of Shakespeare's lovers is also precipitated by an accident—the detention of the message-bearing friar. The student of esthetics, recognizing another kind of logic in art than that of mathematical cause-and-effect, may however conclude that Catherine's death, like that of Juliet, shows a kind of artistic inevitability. Except by a large indirection, the war does not kill Catherine any more than the Veronese feud kills Juliet. But in the emotional experience of the novel, Catherine's dying is directly associated and interwoven with the whole tragic pattern of fatigue and suffering, loneliness, defeat and doom, of which the war is itself the broad social manifestation. And one might make a similar argument about *Romeo and Juliet*.

In application to Frederic and Catherine, the phrase "star-crossed lovers" needs some qualification. It does not mean that they are the victims of an actual malevolent metaphysical power. All their crises are caused by forces which human beings have set in motion. During Frederic's understandably bitter ruminations while Catherine lies dying in the Lausanne hospital, fatalistic thoughts do, quite naturally, cross his mind. But he does not, in the end, blame anything called "Fate" for Catherine's death. The pain of her labor reminds him that her pregnancy has been comfortable and apparently normal; the present biological struggle is perhaps a way of evening things up. "So now they got her in the end. You never got away with anything." But he immediately rejects his own inference: that is, that her sufferings in labor are a punishment for sinful pleasures. Scientifically considered, the child is simply a by-product of good nights in Milan—and there is never a pretence that they were not good. The parents do not happen to be formally married; still, the pain of the child-bearing would have been just as it is even if they had been married fifty times. In short, the pain is natural, inevitable, and without either moral or metaphysical significance. The anonymous "they" is nothing but a name for the way things are.

A little later Frederic Henry bitterly compares the human predicament first to a game and then to a swarm of ants on a log in a campfire. Both are homely and unbookish metaphors such as would naturally occur to any young American male at a comparable time. Living now seems to be a war-like game, played "for keeps," where to be tagged out is to die. Here again, there is a moral implication in the idea of being caught off base—trying to steal third, say, when the infield situation and the number of outs make it wiser to stay on second. "They threw you in and told you the rules and the first time they caught you off base they killed you." One trouble, of course, is that the player rarely has time enough to learn by long experience; his fatal error may come in the second half of the first inning, which is about as far as Catherine seems likely to go. Even those who survive long enough to learn the rules may be killed through the operation of chance or the accidents of the game. Death may, in short, come "gratuitously" without the slightest reference to "the rules."

It is plainly a gratuitous death which comes to the ants on the burning log in Frederic's remembered campfire. Some immediately die in flame, as Catherine is now dying. Others, like Lieutenant Henry, who has survived a trench-mortar explosion, will manage to get away, their bodies permanently scarred, their future course uncertain—except that they will die in the end. Still others, unharmed, will swarm on the still cool end of the log until the fire at last reaches them. If a Hardyan President of the Immortals takes any notice of them, He does little enough for their relief. He is like Frederic Henry pouring water on the burning campfire log—not to save the ants but only to empty a cup.

Catherine's suffering and death prove nothing except that she should not have become pregnant. But she had to become pregnant in order to find out that becoming pregnant was unwise. Death is a penalty for ignorance of "the rules": it is also a fact which has nothing to do with rule or reason. Death is the fire which, in conclusion, burns us all, and it may singe us along the way. Frederic Henry's ruminations simply go to show that if he and Catherine seem star-crossed, it is only because Catherine is biologically double-crossed, Europe is war-crossed, and life is death-crossed.[5]

Notes

4. The *Romeo and Juliet* comment is quoted by Edmund Wilson in "Ernest Hemingway: Bourdon Gauge of Morale," which first appeared in the *Atlantic Monthly* 164 (July 1939), pp. 36–46. The essay was collected in *The Wound and the Bow*, New York, 1941, and reprinted by J. K. M. McCaffery, ed., *Ernest Hemingway, The Man and His Work*, New York, 1950, pp. 236–257. Further page-references to this essay will be to the McCaffery reprint only.

In *A Farewell to Arms* Hemingway was dealing imaginatively but also retrospectively with his own first adult love affair, which had taken place in Milan at the base hospital during his recuperation there in the late summer and autumn of 1918. Harold Loeb alludes to it in *The Way It Was*, New York, 1959, pp. 219–220, stating erroneously that the girl was English. She was in fact Agnes von Kurowsky, an American of Polish ancestry working as a Red Cross nurse. It was she who voluntarily ended the association by letter after Hemingway's return to the United States early in 1919. I am indebted for materials documenting this episode to Mr. J. C. Buck. The portrait of Catherine

Barkley appears to have been influenced by Hemingway's recollection of his first wife, Hadley Richardson. His second wife, Pauline Pfeiffer, was delivered of a son by Caesarean section in Kansas City in 1928 while Hemingway was at work on the novel. See his introduction to the illustrated edition of *FTA* (New York, Scribner's, 1948), p. vii. The manner of Catherine's death was perhaps suggested to Hemingway by this experience. But the portrait of Catherine seems to have been founded chiefly on his remembrance of the Red Cross nurse in Milan. Ten years later, when he was readying *The Fifth Column and the First Forty-Nine Stories* for publication, Hemingway directed Maxwell Perkins to change the name of the nurse in "A Very Short Story" from Ag (for Agnes) to Luz—on the grounds that the name Ag was libellous. EH to MP, 7/12/38. Perkins complied. It is therefore quite clear, as many have surmised, that the central episode of "A Very Short Story" is connected with the love affair in *A Farewell to Arms*.

5. On Catherine's bad luck, see *FTA*, pp. 342, 350.

PAMELA A. BOKER PRESENTS A PSYCHOANALYTIC READING OF THE NOVEL

Nick Adams's traumatic war experience foreshadows Hemingway's own growing disillusionment in the years that followed 1929, not only with the masculine ideal of war, but with his own grandiose heroic self-image, as can be seen in the early Orpen story. Hemingway's 1929 novel, *A Farewell to Arms*, bears a close resemblance to Hemingway's story fragment about the disillusioned and narcissistically wounded soldier Orpen, who chooses to escape from his own fear of death and his growing disillusionment with war by returning to the comforting embraces of his mother. From the early chapters of the book, Lieutenant Frederic Henry is unable to identify himself with the manly activity of war. He is drawn to spend his leave whoring in Milan rather than hunting in the mountains, and upon his return makes the observation that "it did not matter whether I was there or not"—that the war "seemed to run better while I was away."[56] Frederic Henry feels the war "did not have anything to do with me" (37), and finds the idea of carrying a pistol ridiculous. Furthermore, he has no desire to go to Carpathians where the fighting is. For Frederic Henry, as for Orpen, there is something unreal and distant about war. To be in the midst of the war seems to Frederic to be like acting in a movie. To echo Orpen's words about war: "You had to pretend to like it."

The fact that Frederic Henry needed little incentive to lose confidence in the ideal of war, and the ease with which be comes to view his abstract heroic ideal as a pretense and a fake, suggests that he, like Orpen, initially possessed an abstract conception of idealized heroism, and so has failed to establish a secure identification with a realistic paternal figure. As such, like Orpen, he is vulnerable to the regressive fantasy of falling in love with, or being sexually drawn to, a woman who doubles as the narcissistically gratifying maternal object, thus enabling him to recapture, as Orpen does, his infantile lost paradise.

Like Orpen, to lie wounded and helpless in his hospital bed makes Frederic "feel very young," like "being put to bed after early supper" (68). By physically wounding his hero, Hemingway again repairs in fantasy the adolescent's narcissistic wound, which signifies a blow to the masculine ego, and results in a breakdown between the ego and the paternal ego ideal. This in turn motivates a renewed need for narcissistic gratification that may be fulfilled by a regressive fusion with the good, nurturing mother. Wounding facilitates the Hemingway hero's regressive fantasy for unconditional love. It is not the wound itself, therefore, but this unconscious desire for love that may be identified as the repressed, which continually returns in Hemingway's fiction.

Catherine's desire for Frederic mirrors his own fear of loss and separation. Her sexual promiscuity is motivated by the loss of her fiancé to whom, as she now regrets, she had denied sex before he went off to war, where he was later killed. As she explains to Frederic, "I thought perhaps he couldn't stand it and then of course he was killed and that was the end of it" (19). Thus, both Catherine and Frederic are searching to regain a love object that this time cannot be lost, which implies a wish for total self-annihilation through mutual love.

More conscious of her narcissistic desires than Frederic is of his, Catherine longs for complete fusion with him—to feel "our hearts beating" (92) as one—and for the assurance that he has "never belonged to any one else" (105) but her. Like the perfect nurturing mother, she tells him during their lovemaking that she will "do anything you want. . . . There isn't any me any more" (106). Physically, she makes him "all clean inside and out" (104), symbolically restoring him to a state of infantile purity; and after his wounding, like the good-mother nurse in Hemingway's Orpen story, she embodies his unconscious hope of never having to return to war again.

Frederic Henry's "corruption," or regression to infantile fusion, is made complete with his desertion from the army. Hemingway plays out Frederic's symbolic rebirth through his escape from the Germans into a river from which he finally "crawled out, pushed on through the willows and onto the bank" (227). With this gesture his allegiance to patriarchal society "was washed away in the river along with any obligation. . . . I was through. . . . That life was over" (232–33). Having surrendered to his regressive desires for the nurturing mother, Frederic's infantile needs rise to the surface: "I was not made to think. I was made to cat. My God, yes. Eat and drink and sleep with Catherine" (233). The moral implicit in Frederic Henry's actions is one that corroborates both contemporary studies of gender identity and the most ancient Indo-European folklore; namely, that in a patriarchal civilization love is incompatible with patriarchal social structures, and "peace"—meaning the blissful peace of regressive infantile fusion—can only be won at the expense of the sacrifice of a man's masculine identity and autonomy.[57] To achieve a permanent union with Catherine feels to Frederic as if he had at last "come home," and he confesses: "We could feel alone when we were together, alone against the others" (249).[58] As Freud and others have proposed, however, the lovers may feel entirely "together," but only by maintaining an opposite stance "against the others." This isolation from the world thus represents merely another kind of loss that Frederic Henry embraces in exchange for his feelings of loss and disillusionment about war.

Later, therefore, when secreted in a small Italian hotel with Catherine, and occupied with nothing but the primal activities of eating, sleeping, and lovemaking, Frederic Henry begins to show signs of restlessness and boredom. He avoids reading the paper, which reminds him of his desertion and separation from the outside world; and it begins to dawn on him what the "stakes" (31) of his self-willed narcissistic engulfment in the sexual, maternal female really are. Not only does he "feel like a criminal" (251), but after experiencing a taste of his old masculine autonomy by spending an afternoon fishing with the barman, he confesses to Catherine: "My life used to be full of everything. . . . Now if you aren't with me I haven't a thing in the world" (257).

After the lovers escape across the lake to Switzerland, the symptoms of Frederic's isolation begin to worsen, so that now Catherine too senses his restlessness. "I should think sometimes you would want to see other people besides me" (297), she says to him anxiously. Although he denies his emptiness, the narcissistic Catherine, who seeks to merge her identity with Frederic's, still feels threatened and redoubles her hold on him by attempting to persuade him to let his hair grow long like hers so that "we'd both be alike. . . . I want us to be all mixed up. I don't want you to go away" (299–300). Despite her wish that they both "go to sleep at exactly the same moment" (301), Frederic does not go to sleep, but lies awake in his bed, contemplating his growing feeling of entrapment. Through the character of Frederic Henry, in *A Farewell to Arms*, Hemingway explores the ambivalence between the desire to indulge in narcissistic and regressive patterns of behavior in order to escape from his feelings of grief, and his awareness of the dangers of such behavior.

It is impossible to say for certain what led to Hemingway's final decision to kill off Catherine and her baby during childbirth, thereby setting Frederic Henry free from what was originally his refuge from the burden of military heroism. Perhaps it was his own unconscious struggle to assert his masculine autonomy against the marvelous but dangerous comforts of narcissistic, or regressive, maternal fusion and sexual indulgence; or perhaps it was a fictional act of revenge on the procreative-phallic woman and her latest offspring.[59] On a much more fundamental level, however, it is also possible that as a staunch and defensive champion of patriarchal civilization, Hemingway simply could not envision an alternative scenario within the possibilities allowed by Western culture that would enable Frederic and Catherine to live contentedly in isolation from, in Freud's words, "the surrounding world." Hemingway also may have realized that love and sex, particularly regressive, narcissistically based love, do not provide a permanent catharsis for grief; that like gambling, patriotism, drinking, and not-thinking, they are merely temporary anesthetics against disillusionment and loss, and so in time must be given up, albeit reluctantly.

A number of Hemingway's critics have suggested that the rain outside the hospital, through which Frederic Henry walks at the end of the novel, symbolizes his unvoiced feelings about Catherine's death. I would alter this interpretation slightly by proposing that the falling rain represents the tears of grief that Frederic Henry is *unable* to shed himself. In what has been called the omitted "religious" ending to the novel, Hemingway writes: "Blessed are the dead that rain falls on, I thought. Why was that?"[60] Hemingway's phrasing calls to mind the Mosaic Law, which Twain employs more directly in *The Adventures of Tom Sawyer* as a metaphor for his own taboo against grief: "Blessed are those who mourn, for they shall be comforted." Perhaps what Hemingway had in mind in his alternative construction of Frederic's thoughts was this: blessed are those who, like the rain, can cry tears of grief, for they, through their open expression of mourning, can find meaning in death, and thereby find comfort for their loss.

In both the published version of the novel's ending, and a number of the unpublished versions, Frederic finds saying good-bye to the dead Catherine to be "like saying good-by [*sic*] to a statue" (332). In one of the omitted endings in which this sentence occurs, Frederic returns to Catherine's death-bed one last time to see if he could find an emotion to fill the void that he feels; but, as he admits in the published ending, "it wasn't any good" (332). Because Frederic Henry cannot openly express or acknowledge his grief, he must suffer the more devastating loss to the self that results from repressing one's emotions, and mourn eternally, not only for the beloved whom he has lost, but for the *nada* of his own inner emotional emptiness.

Notes

56. Ernest Hemingway, *A Farewell to Arms*, 16–17. All subsequent citations from *A Farewell to Arms* refer to this edition.

57. Jean Markale also points out, in *Women of the Celts*, that in the mythical tales of Diarmaid and Grainne, and Tristan and Isolde, the stale hero's act of falling in love is seen as a trap that permanently draws him away from the social and legal laws and institutions of patriarchal civilization, and labels him as a disloyal, treasonous criminal. The sexual union of Troilus and Cressida, and Othello and Desdemona, according to Janet Adelman in *Suffocating Mothers: Fantasies of Maternal Origin in Shakespeare's Plays*, "*Hamlet*" to "*The Tempest*," signifies an engulfing and "dangerous return to the infant's first union with a nurturing maternal figure" (53) that destroys the hero's masculine identity, itself originally founded on the loss of the maternal figure.

58. About Catherine, Carlos Baker observes that for Frederic Henry: "Where she is, home is . . ." (*The Writer as Artist*, 112).

59. While Hemingway was writing the end of *A Farewell to Arms* his second wife, Pauline, gave birth to his son, Patrick, after a difficult labor and finally an emergency Cesarean section. See Meyers's *Hemingway: A Biography*, 208.

60. While it is impossible to say how many different versions of the ending to *A Farewell to Arms* Hemingway imagined, several alternative endings are preserved in the Hemingway archives at the John F. Kennedy Library in Boston.

THOMAS STRYCHACZ ON THE THEATRICALITY OF WAR

A common idiom speaks of a "theater of war."[1] The phrase refers to the scene of action; the place where martial operations are undertaken. Building on that original image, the twentieth century has added other terms: the "show," staging operations, a "circus," acts of war, the European Theater, and so on. But in what ways could war be said to be theatrical? Because movements of soldiers and armaments and the battles in which they will be employed are scripted, or directed, by generals who remain behind the scenes, taking no hand in the stage-action itself? Because war operations are obsessively watched, depending for their successful outcome on the quality of visual information obtained? Because such obsessive watching transforms terrain into a kind of arena? Because, as in all theater, actions undertaken under the eyes of others somehow liberate a superabundance of meaning, so that these are not simply men fighting but men fighting *for* (their country, freedom, each other, their pride)? The issue is worth pondering because in many respects Hemingway's war stories appear to have little to do with theatricality. . . . Hemingway's war characters, moreover, tend to be men "in the trenches" far removed from the supposedly all-seeing generals who direct the show. Frederic Henry's wounding, which many Hemingway critics and biographers interpret as a re-telling of *the* seminal experience of Hemingway's life, comes apropos of nothing: "I ate the end of my piece of cheese and took a swallow of wine. Through the other noise I heard a cough, then came the chuh-chuh-chuh-chuh—then there was a flash, as when a blast-furnace door is swung open."[3] The action that takes place is unscripted, meaningless; the shell is flung blindly; beyond the mere fact of the Austrian artillery having observed the enemy lines, there is no sense that an audience makes a difference to unfolding events. And, certainly, no one witnesses whatever there is to be seen when Frederic Henry "felt myself rush bodily out of myself."

Subsequent pages, however, return Henry to life amid a series of oddly drawn poses. The following exchange, for instance, takes place with the British ambulance driver who helps him:

> "They tell me you're an American."
> "Yes."
> "I'm English."
> "No!"
> "Yes, English. Did you think I was Italian?" (61–62)

Henry, having already referred to the man as the "Britisher" (61), does not think of him as Italian, and his "No!" is a piece of comic sarcasm that we understand but the Britisher misses. (The Britisher also pats Gordini's shoulder, missing the fact that it is smashed.) Within a few sentences, however, the Britisher, trying to get Henry early treatment, puts his faculty of misinterpretation to different use:

> "Here is the American Tenente," he said in Italian.
> "I'd rather wait," I said. "There are much worse wounded than me. I'm all right."
> "Come, come," he said. "Don't be a bloody hero."

Henry's deadpan presentation of this exchange encourages multiple interpretations. The Britisher reads his protestations as an excessive self-dramatization—though it is unclear whether the Britisher thinks of Henry as being truly heroic at an inappropriate moment (he is being unnecessarily stoic), or simply falsely heroic at an appropriate moment (the moment calls for stoicism, but the man does not believe him).

Henry's actual words could be taken either way. "I'd rather wait" sounds genuine enough, but it is followed by "There are much worse wounded than me," which is certainly true, but smacks enough of the realm of comic-book heroes for the Britisher to perceive it as a merely rhetorical exercise. "I'm all right" is patently untrue. But that last response does allow Henry to claim kinship with the man who has quietly provided a role model for him throughout this whole scene: Gordini. Gordini, "white and sick" after his shoulder was smashed, brings the Britisher for Henry so that the Tenente can have his injuries treated first; "wince[s] and smile[s]" when the Britisher pats his shoulder; and, in response to Henry's question, says "I am all right" (which Henry repeats in his very next speech). Smiling through his pain and caring for Henry first, Gordini cuts a more heroic figure than Henry, who quite unstoically berates his (also wounded) bearers when falling shells cause them to drop him ("If you drop me again";

"You sons of bitches"). We might then read Henry in this passage as neither heroically trying to defer his treatment nor quite posing as a hero but as someone who, by imitating Gordini, tries to reproduce an appropriately heroic role. The Britisher's admonishment to not "be a bloody hero" suggests that Henry's masquerade is still evident. The narrative frame for this moment provides additional evidence: it is preceded by Henry pretending not to know that the Britisher is British, and followed by the Britisher introducing him to the surgeons under aliases: "He is the legitimate son of President Wilson"; "The only son of the American Ambassador."

The scene of Henry's wounding, which begins with a completely unscripted event and ends with Henry posing or at least learning how to pose properly, adds a crucial dimension to the idea of a theater of war in Hemingway's work. Theaters of war set up exemplary situations in which soldiers, under extreme duress, demonstrate (or fail to demonstrate) that they are men. . . .

On the one hand, the "Show" shows what males are made of; it makes males into men by allowing them to represent themselves appropriately; and acts of representation are necessary because the true nature of men cannot be known until put to the test. Manhood, it seems, must be shown to be known. On the other, imputations of theatricalized warfare can he discarded on the grounds that the true nature of men, being interior and somehow always and already present, cannot be conflated with or be contingent on the external display that brings it into being. The scholarly understanding of Hemingway's theater of war has typically been a beautifully wrought paradox: the true nature of men calls into being the acts of representation that are necessary for revealing the true nature of men.

But Hemingway's two great war novels, *A Farewell to Arms* and *For Whom the Bell Tolls*, insist on exploring the full metaphoric weight of "theater of war" and in so doing problematize in a rather different way from his critics the relationship between manhood and war. In the earlier novel, Frederic Henry's various masquerades, of which the scene with the Britisher is only one, suggest that war does indeed allow males to represent manhood. But *Farewell* never loses sight of the theatricality of such representations. And its theaters of war compose an ambiguous analysis of the dramatizations war enforces and of the self-dramatizations war reveals, urging us to explore the possibility that war metaphorizes the acts of self-representation males undertake when not at war. *For Whom the Bell Tolls*, however, demands a very different analysis. The later novel depicts a situation all too familiar to the later twentieth century: a crisis of encroaching totalitarianism figured in unidentifiable systems of power and ruled by an invisible master-eye signifying fantasies of absolute domination. The novel is as magisterial an inquiry into the Western fascination with the dominating (male) gaze and with military intelligence as Luce Irigaray's *Speculum of the Other Woman* (1985) and Michel Foucault's *Discipline and Punish* (1977). Theater—and in particular the many instances of "cave theater" that characterize Robert Jordan's attempts to gain control of the guerrilla band—allows a trenchant critique of the fascist gaze, not so much because it offers a potent strategy of resistance but because it subjects the exercise of male power to a human audience.

Notes

1. According to the *Oxford English Dictionary*, the term "theater" was used to designate the scene of a non-dramatic action as far back as the sixteenth century, though usage in something like its modern form seems to date from the nineteenth century. Mendel in his *Art of War* (1879), for instance speaks of the "theater of operations of an army."

3. Ernest Hemingway, *A Farewell to Arms* (New York: Scribner's, 1929), 58. This work will hereinafter be cited parenthetically by page number in the text.

ALEX VERNON ON THE TERMS *MARITAL* AND *MARTIAL*

In 1978 Judith Fetterley's pioneering book of feminist criticism, *The Resisting Reader*, boldly challenged the macho Hemingway mystique:

> If we weep reading [*A Farewell to Arms*] at the death of
> soldiers, we are weeping for the tragic and senseless waste
> of their lives; we are weeping for them. If we weep at
> the end of the book, however, it is not for Catherine but
> for Frederic Henry. All our tears are ultimately for men,
> because, in the world of *A Farewell to Arms* male life is
> what counts. And the message to women reading this
> classic love story is clear and simple: the only good woman
> is a dead one, and even then there are questions. (71)

Fetterley's book arrived during the salad days of feminist literary criticism, and the deep misogyny she finds in Hemingway, necessary in its day, has since been ameliorated in the criticism. One still finds, however, such antagonistic assertions as Margaret Higonnet's, that Hemingway's image of soldiers appearing pregnant when "protecting their cartridges under their capes" in *A Farewell to Arms* is an "aggressive masculinist metaphor" (215) that wrongly appropriates feminine imagery. Following Nancy Huston, Jennifer Haytock's more sympathetic essay in the *Hemingway Review* concludes that the novel's opening imagery symbolizes how the "soldiers will give birth not to a living being but to violence and death" (70).

Images and talk of pregnancy, childbirth, and marriage in Hemingway have received much critical attention. As generally interpreted, they indicate his male characters' fear of losing independence, freedom, and the pleasures of male camaraderie—their refusal, in other words, to grow up and accept adult responsibilities. I would like to suggest that these images and this discourse also can be directly linked to war.

One way to read the scene of the soldiers marching with "the two leather cartridge boxes on the front of their belts, gray leather boxes heavy with the packs of clips of thin, long, 6.5 mm. cartridges, bulged forward under the capes so that the men, passing on the road, marched as though they were six months gone with child" (4) is as an expression of their male experiencing of the military and war as emasculating and thus feminizing, insofar as the soldier's loss of agency. Their story becomes one of "being done to," to use Samuel Hynes's phrase in *The Soldiers' Tale* with its apt subtitle, Bearing *Witness to Modern War* (3; emphasis added). The male soldier is "done to" not only by the enemy and by the new technology, he also becomes an instrument for and an object of the warmakers on his own side, a victim bearing the burden for empowered others, as the image depicts. Here Reynolds summarizes Hemingway's experience of childbirth through 1922:

> Hemingway grew up with an unusual awareness of a woman's painful and bloody birthing process. Early, before he understood sex and death, he was marked by birth's pain and its accompanying screams. His mother, Grace, continued bearing children until she was forty-three and he was fifteen; at age eleven, Ernest was present when Grace bore his sister Carol at the summer cottage. His father specialized in obstetrics in his home office; all his early life Ernest lived in the presence of pregnant women who carried the secret and suffered the pain. That woman [he saw] birthing on the Andrianople road brought it all back to him, the mystery and the pain. Nowhere in his later fiction would babies ease gently into this world. (*Paris* 77)

To depict a soldier six months gone with child, then, is hardly an envious appropriation of the feminine; it is instead a rendering of the man's position as soldier as one of severe suffering—of the suffering to come as their metaphoric burden approaches term in range of the enemy's guns.

If pregnancy and childbirth for women signify and embody their social bonds, military service signifies a man's social bonds. Paradoxically, military service—and especially for American men headed to the Great War—serves as a liberation from domestic, social obligations and a reassertion of manly autonomy but also as the ultimate tie to society, one that demands the selfless sacrifice of the individual for society. If, as Nina Baym and other feminist scholars have maintained, woman for the male psyche represents social integration, responsibility, and self-sacrifice for the community (through marriage),[18] then she also embodies that very social contract that got him to the battlefield—a symbolic fact that, again, must affect his relations with her. War poster after war poster depicted women (and children) as the motivating spirit calling the soldier to arms; the woman figure was often draped in the American flag. In the foreground of a 1918 poster from the Liberty Loan Committee of Washington, troops in various uniforms bearing their rifles at port arms with bayonets fixed march toward the viewer, and above them the image of a mother holding a child merges into the American flag.[19] Another poster features a female figure draped in the flag and pointing to a roll call of dead soldiers. Anthropological evidence reveals that in some premodern warring cultures, "a man cannot be called a man *or marry* until he has proven himself in battle" (Goldstein 274; emphasis added). But for two transposed letters, *marital* and *martial* are the same word.

Thus Nick Adams in "Night before Landing," on a ship on his way to war, discusses marriage, the story ending the night before landing with Nick's pronouncement about his girl, "We're going to get married" (*Nick* 142). In "Now I Lay Me," Nick in a tent during the war remembers his wounding and fights sleep to fight death, the story concluding with his conversation with another soldier, again, about marriage. And in that originating Nick Adams story "Indian Camp," the young Nick associates childbirth with the husband's death and with a crippling leg injury similar enough to Hemingway's own war wound; to the degree that Hemingway volunteered for ambulance duty, his wound, like the Indian husband's wound and subsequent death, was self-inflicted. Frederic Henry also conceives his child with Catherine Barkley on his hospital bed, once again suggesting an association between fatherhood and war wounds. When at the end of "Big Two-Hearted River" the young Nick tells himself he will never die, his association of the child's birth with the father's death might imply that Nick really is telling himself he will never become a father.[20]

"Rather than being a study in war, love or initiation," wrote Michael Reynolds in *Hemingway's First War: The Making of "A Farewell to Arms,"* the novel "is more properly a study in isolation. Frederic's progression in the novel is from group participation to total isolation" (271). Nick Adams's solo journey in "Big Two-Hearted River" portrays another veteran seeking escape from social allegiance. For an American male to escape war, he must escape social ties. He must, like Harold Krebs and Frederic Henry, desire to relinquish love. Elsewhere Reynolds reports on a correspondence between Owen Wister, the father of the western genre, and Hemingway's editor Maxwell Perkins. *Farewell's* "flaw," as Reynolds paraphrases Perkins, "is that the war story and the love story do not combine. . . . If only the war were in some way responsible for the nurse's death in childbirth" (*1930s* 4–5). The war, I contend, is entirely responsible. Catherine Barkley and the baby both must die at the end of *A Farewell to Arms* not because "for Hemingway the only good woman is a dead one" as Fetterley argues (71), but because for Frederic Henry to have a final farewell to arms, he must lose all obligatory social ties, must escape the social contract embodied in wife and child, just as in an older American tale Rip Van Winkle escapes his henpecking wife and, simultaneously and ironically, the War of Independence.[21]

Another source, then, for a misogynist strain in Hemingway and in other veterans is this symbolic association of women with society and therefore as the cause for the soldier's wartime suffering. The association of children with social responsibility also contributes a misopedist strain, so that the presence of childbirth in Hemingway's war stories signifies what sends the male soldier to war as well as what the emasculated soldier must bear during war. And thus, as Susan Griffin observes, "*So much childbirth in Hemingway's stories. Especially in his war stories*" (319, italics in original). Publications like the *Ladies' Home Journal* and posters and articles exhorting men to defend their homes, their women and children, reinforce the association. The male soldier, especially during World War I, finds himself—to use a literary metaphor from World War II—in a Catch-22. To escape the emasculating nature of the industrializing, bureaucratic new twentieth-century world, he escapes in literature to the western frontier and to Tarzan's Africa,[22] and in life to the war—but the military and the war actually subvert the possibility for autonomous agency and self-definition. One is subject to the desires of the chain of command and subjected to the efforts of the enemy. One is bound to the military family as well as to the social family that the military serves. Hemingway in particular, with his ambiguous soldierly status and his wounding, his confrontation with homosexuality and the dissolution of women's gender roles and prescriptions, hardly discovers in war a buttress for his masculine sense of self.

Notes

18. Baym's "Melodramas of Beset Manhood." See also Laura Mulvey's idea of the "split hero" motif in the western film genre (*Visual and Other Pleasures*). "The Short Happy Life of Francis Macomber" fits Mulvey's scheme, with Macomber the integration-function character and Wilson the resistance-function character, and Margaret Macomber the woman on whom the male split-function conflict turns. See also Jane Tompkins, *West of Everything*.

19. The text below the artwork reads: "For the SAFETY OF WOMANHOOD / For the PROTECTION OF CHILDHOOD / For the HONOR OF MANHOOD / And for LIBERTY THROUGHOUT THE WORLD." This image can be seen at the Provincial Museum of Alberta's online exhibit "The Poster War: Allied Propaganda Art of the First World War" (© 1999) http://www.pma.edmonton.ab.ca/ vexhibit/warpost/english/post29.htm.

20. In the short early poem "Killed Piave—July 8—1918" (1921), Hemingway's narrator, killed at the place and time of Hemingway's wounding, transforms the woman he loved into the bayonet lying with him in his coffin so that sleeping with the woman becomes sleeping with the bayonet (*Complete Poems* 35).

21. For related discussions of Rip Van Winkle, see Fetterley (1–9), Limon (9–13), and Fiedler (25–26). Baym does not explicitly mention war narratives. She cites *For Whom the Bell Tolls* as one novel by a prominent male author that refuses to "reproduce such a scheme" (73).

22. Appropriately, given the connection between the "woman problem" and the rise of both the western and the war novel in the early 1900s, Owen Wister provided a publicity blurb for *Farewell*, and later Hemingway and Wister met and became friends.

RICHARD FANTINA ON CATHERINE AS A HEMINGWAY WOMAN

Catherine suffers from loss and feels isolated since the death of her fiancée, killed at the front in the battle of the Somme. She attaches herself to Frederic to ease the sense of grief and guilt. She experiences guilt because she had denied sex to her boyfriend despite his entreaties in the period just before his death. In a very real sense, she uses Frederic to compensate for this loss. Her suffering is so great that she's willing to submerge herself into a single identity with him as if to diffuse the pain. Throughout the novel, she professes her undying love for Frederic and he reciprocates but Catherine engulfs his identity into her own. As Eby points out, "Catherine's plea is a demand for *recognition* and an attempt, however lovingly expressed, to commandeer her lover's body" (original emphasis 206). She makes numerous statements regarding the merging of her identity with Frederic's, such as: "There isn't any me. I'm you. Don't make a separate me." (111) and "We're the same one" (285). Remarks such as these disguise the fact that it is Frederic who surrenders himself to Catherine, after initially trying to resist falling in love with her. As narrator, he often speaks of Catherine's courage and at one point he says, "If people bring so much courage to the world the world has to kill them to break them so of course it kills them. . . . It kills the very good and the very gentle and the very brave impartially" (239). These words foreshadow Catherine's fate. Hemingway also endows Catherine with one of his most important male characteristics—the ability to face death without fear. As she lays dying, Catherine tells a weeping Frederic, "I'm not afraid. I just hate it" (315). Hemingway reverses stereotypical, gender-specific character traits—in this case, courage and tears. Courage constitutes the single most important element of the Hemingway code hero and here Catherine embodies this virtue while Frederic weeps helplessly. Sandra Whipple Spanier asks, "Why has Catherine, the only character besides Frederic who inhabits this novel from beginning to end, been so consistently ignored as a model of the Hemingway code?" She answers her question with: "The simplest explanation is that it probably never occurred to most readers that the 'code hero' could be a woman"[14] (13).Hemingway invests Catherine with the masculine qualities that he considers essential and that he gives these attributes to a woman demonstrates how he consciously subverts traditional values.

Hemingway's creation of the character of Catherine Barkley has received criticism for its lack of depth. Spanier remarks that Catherine "has been attacked or dismissed for her simplicity" (14) but adds that "the code hero usually *is* a simple character" (14). Although Hemingway never develops Catherine's character fully enough, depriving the reader of the opportunity to better understand her psychology, she possesses certain traits that establish her in the Hemingway *oeuvre* almost as a code hero in her own right. She conforms to other "lost generation" types that Hemingway depicted throughout the 1920s. She experiences the same sense of loss and emptiness. Her boyfriend has been killed, she has lost her religion, and feels no ties to her native England. She appears just as emotionally adrift as Jake Barnes and Brett Ashley in *The Sun Also Rises*. She meets Frederic Henry and essentially takes over his life. In many ways, Frederic's motives, though he acts as narrator, remain as vague as Catherine's. His chief drive, aside from self-preservation, consists of his love for Catherine. When she tells him, "We're the same one" (285), she imposes a unity onto their relationship, a unity quite similar to that which both Catherine Bourne and Barbara Sheldon attempt to impose on their husbands in *The Garden of Eden*. In *A Farewell to Arms*, Catherine Barkley tells Frederic, "there's only us two and in the world there's all the rest of them" (134) and Frederic, as narrator, relates: "we were alone together, alone against the others" (238). Both David Bourne and Frederic Henry accept the limits placed upon their social relations and their confinement in interpersonal relationships imposed upon them by the two Catherines. The major difference, apart from the explicit sex of *The Garden of Eden*, lies in Catherine Barkley's lack of participation in the larger world outside of her relationship with Frederic, and Catherine Bourne's determination to involve herself and her husband in the fulfillment of her will in that world in the form of the narrative of their gender transgressions. Frederic, therefore, remains faithful and devoted to Catherine Barkley to the end, while David and Catherine Bourne undergo a traumatic rupture.

Note
14. Sandra Whipple Spanier, "Catherine Barkley and the Hemingway Code," paper presented at NEMLA, Hartford, CT (March 19, 1985). Ernest Hemingway Collection (Kennedy Library, Boston), 13.

JOHN ROBERT BITTNER ON ANTI-FASCIST ELEMENTS IN THE NOVEL

In *A Farewell to Arms*, when Frederic Henry dives into the river and flees both the retreat and the war, the reader is told that "[a]nger was washed away in the river along with any obligation" (*FTA* 232). It is not only a rejection of the conflict of 1917, it is also a rejection of Fascist doctrine. Between the end of the war and 1929—when the Lateran Treaty created Vatican City as an independent state and isolated the Catholic Church from interfering with Fascism—this doctrine espoused an imperial military dictatorship grounded in a collective sacrifice and struggle on behalf of the Fascist state. For Mussolini, Fascism did not "believe in the possibility or utility of perpetual peace," and pacifism (as displayed by Frederic Henry) was a "cloak" for the cowardly who renounced self-sacrifice. Mussolini wrote, "War alone keys up all human energies to their maximum tension and sets the seal of nobility on those peoples who have the courage to face it" (19). In Fascism, there was no place for the subversive potential of a powerful and popular American antiwar novel set in war-torn Italy, with its protagonist of a wounded war medalist who evolves into an individualist and antiwar pacifist and who chooses to reject the war and escape into neutral Switzerland—a country from which in 1902 Mussolini had been expelled because of his association with an organization of revolutionaries.

In addition to the novel's emphasis on the Caporetto retreat, the subtexts in *A Farewell to Arms* were guilty of befouling two of Fascism's most important symbols: a military uniform and the glory of Rome. The military doctrine of Fascism lent itself well to clothing in uniform, not only of the army under Fascism, but also of the hundreds of thousands of juveniles and young adults who became members of the state-sanctioned youth militia organizations.[2] Prominent in the uniform of both the soldiers and the youth was the black shirt, first used by the Italian national poet and aviator war hero Gabriele D'Annunzio during his command of the postwar takeover of the Yugoslavia border town of Fiume. This takeover was carried out by mutinying Italian soldiers dissatisfied with the Treaty of Rapallo provision making Fiume a buffer city between Italy and Yugoslavia.[3] D'Annunzio clad his soldiers in black shirts, symbolizing the heroic days of the war and honoring the laborers of Emilia and of Romagna, the east-central region of Italy where Mussolini was born.[4] Hemingway had earlier made fun of Mussolini and his uniform in the *Toronto Daily Star* article from the Lausanne Conference: "And then look at his black shirt and his white spats. There is something wrong, even histrionically, with a man who wears white spats with a black shirt" (*DT* 255). In *A Farewell to Arms*, Hemingway makes a point of interweaving the symbolism of Frederic's uniform into the story's narrative. When Frederic discards his military uniform, even though a uniform of 1917, he discards an important symbol of postwar Fascist Italy. Hungry, tired, hiding on the train, Frederic thinks to himself: "I would like to have had the uniform off although I did not care much about the outward forms. I had taken off the stars, but that was for convenience. It was no point of honor" (*FTA* 232).

Even more important than the Fascist uniform was the myth of the Roman Empire, invoked so often to instill Italian patriotism that it took on the qualities of a religion. In the March on Rome of 27 October 1927, the Fascist proclamation issued to accompany the event read, "the army of Blackshirts seizes again the mutilated victory and, pointing desperately toward Rome, restores it to the glory of the Capitol." Sayings paying homage to

Rome littered Fascist literature and speeches, and Roman motifs were introduced into Fascist architecture. As Emilio Gentile states, "[T]he myth of Rome was perhaps the most pervasive mythological belief in fascism's entire symbolic universe" (244).[5]

Shortly before he is sent to the hospital in Milan, Frederic Henry makes fun of Rome in a lighthearted discussion with Rinaldi and the major, but the thrust of the major's remarks could apply as much to the Fascist spirit of 1929 as to the Italian front of 1916:

> Italy will return to the splendors of Rome, said the major. I don't like Rome, I said. It is hot and full of fleas. You don't like Rome? Yes, I love Rome. Rome is the mother of nations. It will never forget Romulus suckling the Tiber. What? Nothing. Let's all go to Rome. Let's go to Rome to-night and never come back. Rome is a beautiful city, said the major. The mother and father of nations, I said. Rome is feminine, said Rinaldi. It cannot be the father. Who is the father, then, the Holy Ghost? Don't blaspheme. I wasn't blaspheming. I was asking for information. (*FTA* 76)

As the major doubtless recognizes, Frederic is not really scorning Rome. This is the banter of friends who have been drinking, friends who need release from the tension of the front (the banter is similar to that of drinking friends from rival colleges who mock a great rival). But the real target behind the banter is the ultrapatriotic rhetoric, always implicit, upon which Mussolini and his henchmen depended. For the totalitarian mind, the banter of a Rinaldi and a Frederic Henry would be unacceptable.

Hemingway has Frederic's singer friend Simmons also reflect negatively on Rome. After the retreat, outside of Milan, Simmons offers his help to Frederic, who responds by asking for civilian clothes:

> "You're about my size. Would you go out and buy me an outfit of civilian clothes? I've clothes but they're all at Rome."

"You did live there didn't you? It's a filthy place. How did you ever live there?"

"I wanted to be an architect."

"That's no place for that." (*FTA* 242)

Hemingway, however, goes beyond symbolism by incorporating negative stereotypes about Italians into an exchange between Frederic and Rinaldi, who himself is becoming disillusioned about the war:

"Oh I love to tease you, baby. With your priest and your English girl, and really you are just like me underneath."

"No, I'm not."

"Yes, we are. You are really an Italian. All fire and smoke and nothing inside." (*FTA* 66)

Then there was the Mussolini scowl, seen in photographs and posters throughout Fascist Italy. In his Lausanne Conference dispatch to the *Toronto Daily Star*, Hemingway wrote, "Get hold of a good photo of Signor Mussolini sometime and study it. You will see the weakness in his mouth which forces him to scowl the famous Mussolini scowl that is imitated by every 19 year old Fascisto in Italy" (*DT* 255). The reader in 1929 would have had little trouble retrieving images of the Mussolini scowl when Frederic replies to Rinaldi:

"You are an ignorant foul-mouthed dago."

"A what?"

"An ignorant wop."

"Wop. You are a *frozen-faced* . . . wop." [italics added]

"You are ignorant. Stupid." I saw that word pricked him and kept on.

"Uninformed. Inexperienced, stupid from inexperience." (*FTA* 66)

Finally, during the retreat, when Aymo is shot crossing a field, Frederic and Piani register equally derogatory comments about the Italian military command structure and blame it for the death. For Frederic, the genius of the Italian people is in the art of living, not in the arts of war. He fears a different kind of strength in the Germans.

> "They weren't Germans," I said. "There can't be any Germans over there."
> "Italians," Piani said, using the word as an epithet, "Italiani!" Bonello said nothing. He was sitting beside Aymo not looking at him. . . .
> "Those were Italians that shot," I said. "They weren't Germans."
> "I suppose if they were Germans they'd have killed all of us," Bonello said.
> "We are in more danger from Italians than Germans," I said. "The rear guard are afraid of everything. The Germans know what they're after." (*FTA* 214)

And so did Ernest Hemingway. In part, his target here is Mussolini and the Fascists of the 1920s, who, he could see, had put the Italian people at great peril, once again enticing them from their strengths in the arts of peace into the horrors and absurdities of war. *A Farewell to Arms* had a subtext that Mussolini and his henchmen could perceive.

Notes

2. The Balilla was for boys aged eight to fourteen, and the Avanguardisti for adolescents fifteen to seventeen. The Fascist doctrine pertaining to the *Balilla* and the *Avanguardisti* is found in Mussolini, 270–75. Also see Schuddekopf, 157, for a photograph of youth in uniform.

3. Although Hemingway had been greatly attracted to the romanticism of D'Annunzio, he saw where that romanticism could lead, and he made D'Annunzio the butt of an early (1920–21) satiric three-line poem in which the swashbuckling warrior and writer gets a "kick" from the slaughter in the Great War. See Hemingway, "D'Annunzio," *88 Poems*, 28.

4. Mussolini, who supported D'Annunzio's occupation, later added for himself and senior officers the black felt hat believed to have been adopted from a Romagna puppet named Fagiolino that yielded a large stick and used it to end arguments. The unit adopted the flag and white skull from the Arditi. D'Annunzio's siege lasted from September

1919 until he was ousted in a battle with legionnaires sent by the
Italian government in December 1920. See Monelli, 83.

5. Emilio Gentile, "Fascism as Political Religion," *Journal of
Contemporary History* 25 (1990): 244, qtd. in Neocleous, 66.

Works Cited

Hemingway, Ernest. *A Farewell to Arms*. New York: Scribner's, 1929.

———. *Dateline: Toronto*. Ed. William White. New York: Scribner's, 1985.

———. *88 Poems*. Ed. Nicholas Gerogiannis. New York: Harcourt Brace
Jovanovich, 1979.

———. *The Short Stories of Ernest Hemingway*. New York: Scribner's,
1966.

Hunt, Anthony. "Another Turn for Hemingway's 'The Revolutionist':
Sources and Meanings." *Critical Essays on Ernest Hemingway's* In Our
Time. Ed. Michael S. Reynolds. Boston: G. K. Hall, 1983. 203–17.

Kirkpatrick, Ivone. *Mussolini: A Study in Power*. New York: Hawthorne,
1964.

Monelli, Paolo. *Mussolini: An Intimate Life*. London: Thames and
Hudson, 1953.

Mussolini, Benito. *Fascism: Doctrine and Institutions*. 1935. New York:
Howard Fertig, 1968.

Neocleous, Mark. *Fascism*. Minneapolis: U of Minnesota P, 1997.

Praz, Mario. "Hemingway in Italy." *The Literary Reputation of Hemingway
in Europe*. Ed. Roger Asselineau. New York: New York UP, 1965.
93–123.

Schuddekopf, Otto-Ernst. *Revolutions of Our Time: Fascism*. New York:
Praeger, 1973.

Smith, Paul. *A Reader's Guide to the Short Stories of Ernest Hemingway*.
Boston: G. K. Hall, 1989.

Zucchi, John E. *Italians in Toronto: Development of a National Identity,
1875–1935*. Montreal: McGill-Queen's UP, 1988.

ROBERT E. FLEMING ON THE
CHARACTER ETTORE MORETTI

In his 1942 introduction to *Men at War*, Hemingway provides
. . . insight into the character of those who became heroes
in wartime: "A good soldier does not worry. He knows that
nothing happens until it actually happens and you live your life

up until then. . . . Cowardice, as distinguished from panic, is almost always simply a lack of ability to suspend the functioning of the imagination. Learning to suspend your imagination and live completely in the very second of the present minute with no before and no after is the greatest gift a soldier can acquire" (xxvii). Between 1927 and 1942, Hemingway created a memorable figure who carries this suspension of the imagination to an extreme: Ettore Moretti. In just a few pages, Ettore illustrates the potential psychological danger that the perfect soldier faces—a loss of his humanity.

Judging from the reactions of students, first-time readers of *A Farewell to Arms* are either unimpressed with Ettore or disturbed by him. One set of readers accepts him as a simple braggart, while a minority suggests that he is a coward for concealing the fact that he is an officer and thereby avoiding being singled out by the enemy. Another minority views him with negative feelings that range from disgust to horror for his obvious inhumanity. Nobody seems to agree with Frederic's assessment of Ettore as hero. . . .

Frederic encounters Ettore, an officer he has known previously, while he is in Milan, undergoing treatment for his own war wound. A noncombatant who was accidentally wounded while unheroically eating supper in a dugout, Frederic can bear testimony to the impersonality of modern war, since he and his ambulance drivers are not strategic targets but rather examples of what has come to be termed "collateral damage": they are killed or wounded just because of their proximity to a combat unit. Nevertheless, Frederic stands to be awarded a silver medal for his wound, largely because, like the soldier in "In Another Country," he is an American. Ettore has lived in America with relatives but entered the war in 1915 during a visit to his parents in Torino. . . . Now only twenty-three years old, he is already an experienced veteran of two years of combat.

Ettore teases Frederic about the likelihood of his receiving a medal, observing that "the girls at the Cova will . . . think you killed two hundred Austrians or captured a whole trench by yourself" (121). He also says, "Believe me, I got to work for my medals" (121). While he has been decorated five times,

95

Ettore doesn't take the whole process seriously. He recognizes the political nature of medals, noting that only one of his five medals has cleared the maze of paperwork in the Italian military establishment. When an action is unsuccessful, the decorations are held up, no matter how heroic the actions of the individual soldiers have been. Ettore prefers wound stripes to medals. Unlike medals, wound stripes are issued—not awarded—only to those who have truly been in the thick of the action. As he puts it, "You only get one for a wound that puts you three months in the hospital" (121).

Ettore is combat-wise. He carries a rifle, he says, so that the enemy can't tell that he is an officer. Snipers, as Ettore well knows, chose then—and still choose—to target soldiers who carry only pistols or who carry binoculars. These men are either officers or forward observers for artillery, and their loss will be more significant to the enemy than the loss of a common foot-soldier. For an officer, carrying a rifle is a means of adopting protective coloration, blending in with the men he commands. But the rifle is not mere camouflage for Ettore. He uses it to shoot enemy soldiers, and he seems to do so with considerable enthusiasm. He tells Frederic and some friends about killing the man who gave him one of his own serious wounds, an Austrian who threw a potato-masher grenade at him: "I shot the son of a bitch with my rifle. . . . I shot him in the belly. I was afraid I'd miss if I shot him in the head" (122).

The fact that he gut-shot his opponent does not necessarily establish Ettore as a sadist or sociopath. While a gut shot means a slow, painful death and is considered a serious breach of code among civilian hunters of game, Ettore's observation about being afraid he would miss if he shot for the head is in accord with military training to shoot for the "center of mass": aiming at a soldier's head may result in the bullet going too high. U.S. military marksmanship charts from World War II superimposed a bull's-eye on a Nazi soldier, the center ring covering the stomach; misses that went either high or low were still likely to take the target out of action.

But one of Ettore's auditors is Simmons, an American opera singer who is not involved in the war. As a more humanistic type of man who has never been to the front, Simmons wonders about the wounded Austrian, asking, "How did he look?" The question doesn't seem to register with Ettore, who speculates about why the Austrian threw the grenade, thereby bringing on his own death. Simmons asks again, "How did he look when you shot him?" Ettore's answer—"Hell, how should I know?" (122)—suggests that Ettore will never have bad dreams about the man he killed. The man was an obstacle, but he is one no longer. Ettore seems incapable of empathizing with his dead foe. His lack of remorse suggests that he may be operating on the border of sociopathology. While he is not so bloodthirsty as Barker, the pilot (and "bloody murderous bastard") in "The Snows of Kilimanjaro" who disgusts his messmates by telling how he bombed and strafed unarmed Austrian officers on a leave train, Ettore clearly exhibits an asocial personality. Unlike then-colonel Harold G. Moore, writing of the North Vietnamese he and his men had just killed, Ettore does not reflect that "[i]t was a sobering sight. Those men, our enemies, had mothers, too" (Moore 252).

Even more surprising is his indifference to the potential seriousness of his own wounds, the most dangerous of which is in the foot that was hit by the potato-masher grenade. Ettore describes this wound in detail: "There's a dead bone in my foot that stinks right now. Every morning I take new little pieces out and it stinks all the time" (121–22). But his description is detached, almost clinical. Clearly he lacks the imagination to worry about the presence of gangrene or to fear the loss of his leg and even (like Harry in "The Snows of Kilimanjaro") the eventual loss of his life. Instead, Ettore focuses on the material advantages of the war. Already in line for a battlefield promotion to captain, Ettore looks forward to a war long enough to ensure his promotion to colonel; he is, in fact, the only character in the novel to wish that the war will continue indefinitely. . . .

That such men as Ettore really do exist in war is attested to by World War II *Stars and Stripes* cartoonist Bill Mauldin, who coincidentally also served on the Italian front. While Mauldin says in his postwar nonfiction book *Up Front* that it is not common for the soldier to turn into a killer—"No normal man who has smelled and associated with death ever wants to see any more of it" (14)—he notes that there are exceptions to this rule. . . .

Frederic's only attempt to emulate Ettore's amoral approach to war occurs during the disastrous retreat from Caporetto. After one of his ambulances gets hopelessly stuck in the mud while he and his men are fleeing the advancing Austrian army, Frederic orders two sergeants from an engineering unit to help cut brush to put under the wheels. The two men refuse his direct order and set off down the road. Frederic acts as Ettore might have acted under the same circumstances: he draws his pistol—earlier in the novel ridiculed as a useless, inaccurate weapon—and fires three shots, wounding one of the men. So far, he has acted under the stress of a tense combat emergency, but when his driver Bonello proposes, "Let me go finish him" (*FTA* 204), Frederic hands him the reloaded pistol and watches while Bonello attempts to do so. When the pistol does not fire on Bonello's first try, Frederic compounds his guilt by advising him, "You have to cock it" (204). Bonello fires, killing the sergeant. Why does Frederic behave so ruthlessly? Why doesn't he load the wounded sergeant into one of the remaining mobile ambulances? Frederic, who has earlier ignored the antiwar talk of his drivers, seems to have been infected by Ettore's wartime ruthlessness and to have behaved as he feels an officer should behave.

But this scene is in counterpoint to two scenes that follow immediately after it. First, another driver, Bartolomeo Aymo, is killed by the Italian rear guard as Frederic and his drivers, having abandoned the remaining ambulances, hurry to catch up with their retreating army. Even closer to home is Frederic's own near-death experience at the hands of the drumhead court martial at the bridge over the Tagliamento, where he realizes that the rough "justice" being carried out will mean his death. Frederic's cutting off of his officer's insignia and his later changing into Simmons's civilian clothes signify his abandonment of the lessons Ettore's behavior has taught him. Henceforth he will follow the lessons of love taught by Catherine and the priest.

Ettore Moretti provides a negative definition of true heroism. A sort of prefiguration of modern movie androids such as Arnold Schwarzenegger's Terminator, Ettore becomes the perfect killing machine. Unlike a Frederic Henry, a Nick Adams, or a Robert Jordan, Ettore will never be able to imagine—or even to wonder—what another human being may be feeling. While he may be the ideal man for wartime or an ideal follower for a Fascist dictator, Catherine accurately recognizes him for what he is, an incomplete human being whom war can transform into a sort of monster.

Works Cited

Hemingway, Ernest. *A Farewell to Arms*. New York: Scribner's, 1970.

———. *Men at War: The Best War Stories of All Time*. New York: Crown, 1942.

———. *The Short Stories of Ernest Hemingway*. New York: Scribner's, 1961.

Lewis, Robert W. *A Farewell to Arms: The War of the Words*. New York: Twayne, 1992.

Mandel, Miriam. *Reading Hemingway: The Facts in the Fictions*. Metuchen, NJ: Scarecrow, 1995.

Mauldin, Bill. *Up Front*. New York: Henry Holt, 1945.

Moore, Harold G., and Joseph L. Galloway. *We Were Soldiers Once . . . And Young*. New York: Harper Torch, 2002.

Spanier, Sandra Whipple. "Hemingway's Unknown Soldier: Catherine Barkley, the Critics, and the Great War," *New Essays on* A Farewell to Arms. Ed. Scott Donaldson. Cambridge: Cambridge UP, 1990. 75–108.

Wylder, Delbert E. *Hemingway's Heroes*. Albuquerque: U of New Mexico P, 1969.

ELLEN ANDREWS KNODT ON
SHOOTING THE SERGEANT

Most critical attention has focused on Lt. Henry's detention by the Italian battle police, his escape by diving into the Tagliamento, and his subsequent desertion from the army. Much less attention has been paid to incidents of the retreat leading up to these events, particularly Lt. Henry's shooting the Italian sergeant. If the Caporetto retreat provides the key to the novel, then we must also take this scene into account in our interpretations. In fact, I suggest, it is a pivotal scene. Lt. Henry's shooting the sergeant tells us everything about Frederic Henry, everything about the novel, and everything (or at least a great deal) about Hemingway's writing process. . . .

There is no direct comment on how Lt. Henry feels about the shooting, but in the remainder of the scene, he refers twice to seeing the sergeant lying on the road. After trying fruitlessly to get the car out, Lt. Henry thinks, "It was my fault. I had led them up here. The sun was almost out from behind the clouds [thus exposing them to the danger of air attack] and the body of the sergeant lay beside the hedge" (205). As they take the two remaining cars across the field in an attempt to continue their journey, Lt. Henry notes that the two young girls who are also passengers on the ambulances "seemed to have taken no notice of the shooting," and looking back, he sees that "[t]he sergeant lay in his dirty long-sleeved underwear" (206). The last reference to the dead sergeant occurs after the remaining two cars get stuck and the men are on foot. Piani says, "You certainly shot that sergeant, Tenente" (a line which can be read several ways). And Bonello boasts, "I killed him. . . . I never killed anybody in this war, and all my life I've wanted to kill a sergeant" (207). Piani criticizes the way Bonello killed the sergeant "on the sit," and the men discuss what Bonello will say in religious confession (207). The episode regarding the shooting is never mentioned directly again. And yet its significance hovers over the rest of the novel.

Readers interpret this scene consistent with their views of Frederic Henry's character and their overall interpretation of the novel and hold widely divergent views. Some, like Charles Nolan, are unwilling to see Lt. Henry as anything but heroic and justify his actions: "To make Frederic less than heroic is to undercut his character and diminish Hemingway's meaning. . . . [I]t is unlikely that he would have made his protagonist in this, one of his best novels, anything but honorable. Frederic Henry shoots the sergeant because, by the cold logic of war, that is what is required of him" (275).

Others, like James Phelan, are troubled by what they see as mixed messages in the text.[1] Phelan recognizes the problems the shooting scene creates for readers who conclude that Lt. Henry is a hero, but he also characterizes some of Frederic's actions during the initial retreat with the ambulances as "decisive": Frederic leads his men off the main road, decides when they should eat, etc. (Phelan 63). But "problems arise when Frederic reacts to their [the sergeants'] most egregious offense . . . by shooting at them, and wounding one, who is then killed, with Frederic's approval, by Bonello" (64). Phelan raises several questions provoked by this incident: "Does Hemingway want us to see Frederic's response as justified in some way? . . . What is the significance of the placement?" (64). Phelan concludes that "we can be confident that he [Hemingway] does not fully endorse Frederic's reaction here. Given Hemingway's attitudes about the war's destruction, we can infer that killing under these circumstances is clearly overdoing it" (64). Phelan tries to reconcile the contrast between the "decisive" Frederic and the Frederic who shoots the sergeant by saying that this incident is a marker of the change taking place within Frederic Henry (65). . . .

Still other readers, like Scott Donaldson, see Lt. Henry as "untrustworthy" ("Frederic"183).[2] Donaldson explains:

> [T]he lieutenant does not conduct himself bravely or intelligently. . . . During the retreat Lieutenant Henry is given his one chance to command, and makes a botch of it. He orders his three ambulances onto side roads where they bog down permanently. He shoots the uncooperative sergeant to no particular effect for when the others proceed on foot, the lieutenant leads good soldier Aymo to a senseless death and Bonello surrenders to save his skin knowing Frederic will not turn him in. In sum, the Tenente loses his ambulances and all his men but one, and it is—as he reflects—largely his own fault. ("Frederic" 79)

The wide divergence in views from many excellent readers of the novel may stem from a desire to categorize Lt. Henry as one thing or another, heroic or non-heroic, admirable or unreliable, while I think Hemingway's portrait of the lieutenant is more complex, composed of actions both praiseworthy and blameworthy, which create a highly realistic, believable portrait of the architecture student caught up in World War I. Hemingway's 1929 readers, having just experienced their first modern war, might have to ignore or somehow justify shooting the sergeant in order to maintain their belief in Lt. Henry's courage and good character. Contemporary readers, who have been exposed to many more accounts of war, may be more willing to accept that a "good" man, even one who may act with good intentions, may commit foolish, stupid, or even barbarous acts in wartime. Americans in recent times have just experienced the allegations that Vietnam war hero, former U.S. senator, and current university president Bob Kerrey may have participated in killing an entire village of Vietnamese women and children. Hemingway understood that what happens during wars is far more complicated and confusing than neat categorizations or labels can convey. . . .

Shooting the sergeant, as I see it, is a pivotal point in the novel, a "point of no return" for analysis or interpretation of Frederic Henry as protagonist. Is he victim, tragic hero, killer, or all three? How is one to reconcile these (and other) divergent views? What meaning did Hemingway intend to be drawn from these events? . . .

The manuscript versions of Chapter 29 offer tantalizing evidence of Hemingway's intent in a change that he made and then changed back. In the manuscript of *A Farewell To Arms* at the Kennedy Library, the first typescript (made from the handwritten one) has the sentence, "I shot three times and *dropped one*" [my italics]. But in his handwriting Hemingway crossed out "dropped one" and wrote "one fell." The sentence then read, "I shot three times and one fell," emphasizing the more passive image of something simply falling and distancing the shooter from the consequence of the shooting. Also, the phrase "dropped one" sounds more casual and indeed more callous because of its connection to hunting game—the same phrase could be used to report the result of hunting ducks or pheasants, "one" versus "him." (JFK Library Box 64 and 65.4) Since Hemingway chose to restore the original wording of "dropped one" in the final manuscript, he seems to have intended to call attention to the more active, more callous action of the shooter and to make his protagonist responsible for this act.

In addition to the letters and manuscript change, the answer of intent also lies, I think, in Hemingway's attitudes toward the nature of war and war heroes, expressed both from without and within the text of the novel. After his wounding in Italy, the very young Hemingway wrote to his family from his hospital bed in 1918, "There are no heroes in this war" (*SL* 19). And both Reynolds and Donaldson point to a sentence Hemingway wrote on a piece of the *Farewell* manuscript, "The position of the survivor of a great calamity is seldom admirable" (Reynolds 60; Donaldson, "Frederic" 181). Within the text, Frederic Henry himself disavows heroism in his wounding: "I was blown up while we were eating cheese. . . . I didn't carry anybody. I couldn't move" (*FTA* 63). As we have seen, Lt. Henry's actions during the retreat were not noteworthy, certainly not heroic, even prior to the shooting of the sergeant, and not afterward either: he loses Aymo to the Italian "rear guard who are afraid of everything" (214), an echo of his own fears as he shoots the sergeant. I think it was important to Hemingway that Frederic Henry *not* be a hero, but a man caught up in events in love and war that he did not control, and yet also a man who was not merely a blameless victim of events.

When Aymo is killed—probably by Italians, not Germans— Lt. Henry says without intentional irony, "the killing came suddenly and unreasonably" (218); yet the reader should notice that Lt. Henry's shooting the sergeant happens just as suddenly and just as unreasonably. Shooting the sergeant is so important because it underscores the unreasonableness of war and the rarity, if not the impossibility, of heroism. Hemingway uses the word "unreasonably" in connection with Aymo's death, and it is important to the novel that the narrator himself has at least temporarily lost his reason—he is an integral part of the whole absurdity of war, not just a somewhat superior observer. His unreasonable detention at the Tagliamento bridge by the carabinieri does not make up for his own loss of reason in his earlier panic over the stuck cars in the field.

While the two events seem linked in Hemingway's echo structure, one could argue here that the executions of officers by the carabinieri show unreason carried to its ultimate absurdity. There is, after all, at least some justification for Lt. Henry's asking the sergeants to stay and cut brush in order to try to move the ambulances and avoid being the target of enemy airplanes. Their refusal to help may not have justified summary execution, but there is an issue here. The case of the execution of Italian officers at the Tagliamento bridge seems totally unreasonable without any testimony or evidence of any sort. Nevertheless, both incidents underscore war's irrationality.

Lt. Henry tries to apply reason in the railroad car after he pulls himself from the river, arguing that his obligation to the war is finished: "You had lost your cars and your men as a floorwalker loses the stock of the department in a fire" (232). But his analogy seems self-deceiving because the floorwalker did not presumably make the decisions that caused the fire, and Lt. Henry already has acknowledged that he was at fault for the decisions that cost him the cars and the men. Hemingway subtly underscores Lt. Henry's failure by having the lieutenant notice earlier "two British ambulances" in the line of vehicles at the bridge over the Tagliamento, which Piani tells him come from Gorizia (their starting point), whereupon Lt. Henry says, "They got further than we did" (220).

In the remainder of the novel, Hemingway further underscores the futility of war and lack of reason in his glancing reference to Henri Barbusse's *Le Feu* (1916) as Lt. Henry and Count Greffi talk over billiards (261). In the introduction to his later work *Men at War* (1942), Hemingway writes that Barbusse "was the first one to show us . . . that you could protest, in anything besides poetry, the gigantic useless slaughter and lack of even elemental intelligence in generalship . . . of that war . . ." (xvi). As William Dow remarks, Hemingway and

Barbusse "create a world of suffering and absurdity in which natural events and humanity's irrational actions collide" (82). It seems to me that when Lt. Henry shoots the sergeant we have a perfect picture in miniature of natural events and irrational actions colliding. If one agrees with Michael Reynolds that "[u]ltimately, Caporetto stood for the entire war experience, and that experience was defeat. . . . a defeat of the spirit . . . which informs the action of *A Farewell to Arms*" (282), then Frederic Henry's shooting the sergeant is an integral part of that defeat and that action.

Notes
1. See also Jeffrey Walsh (57) for discussion of the difficulties presented by this scene.
2. See also Gerry Brenner (35) and Margot Norris, who see Hemingway as deliberately creating an unreliable narrator as a rhetorical manipulation of his readers.

KEITH GANDAL ON HEMINGWAY AND ETHNICITY

If Hemingway felt himself in such profound competition with ethnic Americans for status in the military, as I am claiming, one would expect this sense of rivalry to arise in some manner in his other major post–World War I fictions, especially his novel of the Great War. And, indeed, as we saw at the very start of this study, *Sun* is not the only Hemingway novel of the era in which an Anglo narrator experiences an antagonistic sense of competition with an ethnic American. In *A Farewell to Arms*, published 3 years later, the reprised theme is a minor one, but, interestingly, in this novel it is absolutely blatant rather than slightly subtle (as it is in *Sun*). In the war novel, this theme of competition with ethnic Americans for military status and women is treated directly; in addition, the issue of the ethnic American being promoted on the basis of "merit" is explicitly raised.

We are now in a better position to appreciate the details of that sequence. Again, Anglo narrator Frederic Henry finds himself locking horns with an Italian American, Lieutenant

Ettore Moretti, who challenges Henry's right to his decorations. Importantly, Moretti, like Cohn, is ill-mannered and arrogant; he is "conceited" and "bored everyone he met"; again like Cohn, who has the American military training stamp on him and so doesn't drink much and maintains a chivalrous propriety with women, Moretti, though he is in the Italian Army, is "no boozer and whorehound." "I don't drink and I don't run around," he asserts; he "know[s] what's good" for him in the eyes of the military (88–91), and, though the concern with temperance and chastity is much more of a concern of the moralistic American Army than the Italian Army, Moretti also has his eye on an American military career. In any case, Moretti's resemblance to the U.S. Army's "new man" makes sense: Hemingway's major quarrel is with the American Army, not the Italian one.

It seems hardly coincidental that this challenge to Henry comes, not from one of the many Italian soldiers in the book, but one of the two Italian Americans who make an appearance. My claim is that Hemingway felt in competition with ethnic Americans, not with foreigners (and thus, likewise, Jake is jealous that Brett sleeps with Cohn, but actually helps her bed Romero, even though that latter liaison destroys Jake's relationships with the other bullfighting aficionados). Because they pose no threat to Henry's sense of his status, the Italians are much more appealing to Henry than this Italian American; to take one small example, just a few pages after the uncomfortable sequence with conceited and boring Moretti, Henry encounters, by contrast, two "Italians [who] were full of manners" (96).

And part of my contention is that Hemingway specifically felt in competition with ethnic Americans over status in the U.S. Army. Thus it is also significant that *A Farewell to Arms* makes clear that Moretti would achieve higher rank than Henry in the American Army as well as the Italian one because he is not only a seasoned soldier and "legitimate hero" (91) but in addition a bilingual speaker. Thus Moretti's question to Henry—"Why don't you go in the American Army?" (90)—is hardly casual for Henry, or Hemingway, even though

Henry has already been wounded and the U.S. Army might simply consider him unfit to fight. We can speculate that if Hemingway were to have answered this question during his own Red Cross service in Italy (once the draft age had been dropped and he became eligible for service), his reluctance to join the American Army might have had to do with the fact that in the U.S. military, he would have had to compete with soldiers like Moretti all the time, not just on this odd occasion, and given Moretti's proven competence in combat, plus his language abilities, Hemingway would have found himself at a disadvantage with such ethnic Americans.

Though the ambulance service in Italy is humiliating for Hemingway because Italy is a minor theater of the war and Red Cross ambulance work is hardly soldiering, as an alternative to the American Army, it nonetheless offers the advantage of exempting Hemingway from daily direct competition with ethnic Americans. Anglo Americans, not ethnic Americans, tended to join the Red Cross ambulance corps; moreover, although there were Italian Americans like Moretti who returned to Italy to fight in the Italian Army, they were few and far between. It is also no coincidence that soon after his encounter with Moretti, the subject of American military training camps comes up, and Henry comments, without explaining his reasons, "I was glad I wasn't in a training camp" (100).

In fact, in this context, I would suggest an alternative to the typical interpretation of Hemingway's expatriation after World War I, usually understood in terms of issues raised in a short story such as "Soldier's Home" from *In Our Time*: the trauma of combat and the alienation it produces from those back home unacquainted with war. Hemingway's expatriation in Europe has generally been seen to offer a moral freedom and spiritual camaraderie less available in America. So, in that short story, for example, Krebs feels unable to relate to American women back home after the war. "That was the thing about French girls and German girls. There was not all this talking. You couldn't talk much and you did not need to talk. It was simple and you were friends."[41] But Hemingway's

European expatriation can also be understood as a continuation of his wartime situation in Italy that allowed him to avoid the American "training camps." Expatriation allowed him to continue to avoid the American soldiers, especially the ethnic American soldiers, whom the army sent into battle or promoted and with whom Hemingway felt agonizingly in competition. If Henry's "separate peace," tied up with his ability to no longer "feel insulted" by an elite combat group of "aviators" who take him for a slacker (173), is achieved in *A Farewell to Arms* by heading out of the war zone for Switzerland, Hemingway's postwar "separate peace," involving a similar freedom from humiliation, can analogously be achieved by going back to Europe and leaving behind the domain of American—and ethnic American—soldiers and officers.

The encounter with the ethnic American has an easy, happy resolution in *A Farewell to Arms*, unlike that in *Sun*, perhaps because Hemingway is more confident at the time of its writing, as a result of his literary success, perhaps also because the uncomfortable experience of competition for status during the war is 3 years more remote. He has also had more experience with women, and his uncomfortable experience in 1925 with Lady Duff Twysden (the principal model for Brett), who wouldn't sleep with him but slept with Harold Loeb (the main model for Cohn),[42] has also receded some. In any case, in *A Farewell to Arms*, the British nurse love interest, unlike her counterpart Brett Ashley in the earlier novel, has been made immune to the "charms" of the ethnic American; Catherine Barkley finds Moretti "conceited" and a bore. "We have heroes too," she asserts; "But usually, darling, they're much quieter." (Apparently, the difference between the boring Jewish American Cohn and the boring Italian American Moretti is that Cohn usually says too little and Moretti talks too much.) She is also less captivated by rank and title than Brett: when Henry asks her, in discussing Moretti, "Wouldn't you like me to have a more exalted rank?" she reassures him his rank is sufficient (91–92). It is of course precisely because in this novel the desirable Anglo woman isn't impressed by or attracted to the ethnic American military figure that the issue of competition between the Anglo narrator and the ethnic American can be a minor, momentary irritation and anxiety that never comes to a crisis.

Notes

41. Ernest Hemingway, "Soldier's Home," *In Our Time* (New York: Macmillan, 1986), 72.

42. On the Twysden, Hemingway, Loeb triangle, see Reynolds, *Hemingway: The Paris Years*, 288–291, 297, 300–302.

JACKSON A. NIDAY II AND JAMES H. MEREDITH ON TEACHING *A FAREWELL TO ARMS* TO AIR FORCE CADETS

As with all great literature, what students take away from *A Farewell to Arms* depends to a large degree on what they bring to the text. English teachers who accept that statement as an axiom will most likely allow the following as a theorem: the more similar individual students in a classroom are in terms of their worldviews, the more likely it is that a class's reading of a work will fall short of broadening the intellectual horizons of its individual members. If the theorem holds, a class of military cadets presents one of the more formidable challenges a teacher can face when working with a book like *Farewell*. Though they are not cut from the same bolt (in spite of the fact they dress just alike), students at the U.S. Air Force Academy (USAFA) usually hold strong affinities for words like "patriotism," "honor," "nation," and "duty." Moreover, the most vocal students tend to hold views on human sexual relations that could be described as traditional or conservative. Upon encountering such characters as Frederic Henry and Catherine Barkley, many of these students balk. Whether explicitly or tacitly, they often ask the same question: Why should they devote time and energy to reflect on characters whose values may seem at such odds with their own? . . .

Linked by the topic of loyalty, two themes take center stage with the cadets: Frederic's virtues and vices as a soldier of fortune, and the intimate relationship between Frederic and Catherine Barkley. . . .

For cadets who are taught to hold classical military virtues in the highest regard, Frederic Henry presents a prickly problem. He is an American in the Italian army holding the rank of lieutenant. We pose several questions: What does reading of such a character have to offer a cadet? What sense of dedication or loyalty to this mission could he have? His charge is to drive an ambulance, but he fails to complete his final mission. He then deserts to escape execution for a conviction of treason from a drumhead trial. The discussions of Frederic Henry as soldier focus on his purpose for being in Italy, his competence in performing his duties, and his commitment to the cause for which he volunteered.

A number of questions help the cadets focus on the significance of information that is conspicuous in its absence. What is Henry's purpose? Why is he in Italy? Why is he, as an American citizen, serving in the Italian army? In fiction, narrator silences can be just as telling as narrator or character declarations, even if a definitive conclusion evades us in the silence. The story raises the question of Henry's purpose early in a passage we have students consider in class discussion:

> "How do you do?" Miss Barkley said. "You're not an Italian, are you?"
> "Oh, no."
> Rinaldi was talking with the other nurse. They were laughing.
> "What an odd thing—to be in the Italian army."
> "It's not really the army. It's only the ambulance."
> "It's very odd though. Why did you do it?"
> "I don't know," I said. "There isn't always an explanation for everything."
> "Oh, isn't there? I was brought up to think there was."
> "That's awfully nice." (18)

True, there isn't always an explanation for everything, but for some things we expect explanations. When people have to make conscious choices and exert considerable effort in pursuit of a choice, we expect answers to, "Why did you do it?" The point of interest here is that the narrator is silent on the question.

What does that silence suggest? The question invites serious speculation from students. If the character offers no answer, does it mean he doesn't have an answer or that he is either reluctant or ashamed to state it explicitly? But what does it mean when the narrator offers no explanation? Ostensibly, the narrator has had time to gain a perspective the character could not have had. If he is silent on so pressing a question, are the explanations still missing? Or are they now unimportant? . . .

[Is] Frederic Henry a competent officer? His failures in getting his ambulance entourage to Udine often elicit heated debate among cadets. We focus the discussion with questions such as these: Was the choice to break ranks in the retreat a prudent one for Frederic to make? Whether the cadets answer yes or no, we press them to give their reasons. Did Frederic have the authority to order the errant sergeants to cut brush to free the ambulance wheels from the ruts? Again, we press them for their reasons. Finally, did Frederic have the authority or justifiable reasons to shoot at the sergeants—and to authorize the killing of one? We ask them to look at the story in terms of tone and narrative distance. The incident is related dispassionately. Frederic gives the order. The sergeants refuse to obey. He repeats the order. They flee. He fires on them, hitting one. Bonello executes the wounded sergeant, following Frederic's detailed instructions on how to fire the pistol. The car won't budge. They give up. Then Frederic says, "Better throw the coat away" (206). Following that episode, this same man gives the two tagalong girls each a ten-lira note as he directs them to the nearest main highway. . . .

Is Frederic an officer meting out military justice? Or is he an opportunist whose poor decisions have led to frustration he is unable to manage, climaxing in a senseless murder? What can we make of the instructions to discard the coat? What kind of man orders an execution one moment and offers mercy the next? These questions move us to extend our discussion of

Frederic as leader to Aymo's death and Bonello's desertion. To what degree may those two events be attributed to Frederic's leadership or lack of leadership?

A troubling related theme for the cadets weaves its way through the novel as the narrator returns to it repeatedly. That is, how committed is Frederic to the Italian cause? We have the cadets focus on four passages. The first passage is early in the novel, the one in which a relatively more idealistic Frederic debates with Gavuzzi, Manera, and Passini about what would be required to bring the war to an end. This debate raises some intriguing questions when considered in terms of narrative distance. The character Frederic argues with the others in his most idealistic frame of mind. When we get to the end of the novel, we know that the character's perspective on war, victory, love, and loss has changed radically. Therefore, we ask our cadets what Hemingway is up to here. Do the Italian mechanics offer the implied author's view of the war? Or are their opinions simply a foil for the young Frederic's naïveté?

Midway through the novel, Frederic has been wounded, and he has fallen in love. Now, as he anticipates a return to the front, Frederic shows a different attitude toward things martial. When Gino employs the high rhetoric of patriotism, Frederic the narrator offers us a glimpse inside Frederic the character's head: "Abstract words such as glory, honor, courage, or hallow were obscene beside the concrete names of villages, the numbers of roads, the names of rivers, the numbers of regiments and the dates. Gino was a patriot, so he said things that separated us sometimes, but he was also a fine boy" (185). We ask two questions here. First, what does this contempt for the abstract and esteem for the concrete suggest about the character? Second, why does patriotism bother Frederic, who is a volunteer?

The question of Frederic's commitment takes another turn in the dreamlike internal monologue we get when he's riding with the guns in the flatcar. We ask for a volunteer to read aloud the second, third, and fourth paragraphs of chapter 32. What is most notable in the passage? Most students can feel the difference in the narrator's state of mind that is reflected in the writing's style and tone, but often they have difficulty expressing the difference or knowing what to make of it. To help them grasp and express the significance of those differences, we ask a number of questions: Why does the story change to the second-person "you" here? What does the pronoun tell us when we think about it in terms of narrative distance? What does the shift from the first-person narrator to the second-person voice tell us about what is being said? What does the floorwalker analogy suggest about Frederic at this moment? Is it an apt analogy? These questions provoke active discussion. Obviously, the implied author is adjusting our view. For what purpose? We ask the cadets to consider the moment in Frederic's life and the topic on his mind. How do people experience such moments? How absurd is the situation? To help them see what's happening, we direct them to the passage where Frederic tells Catherine that he feels like a criminal because he's deserted. We assign a one-page thought piece for homework to invite preliminary assessments of Frederic as soldier. What we hope they get at this point is that Frederic is undergoing a profound transformation. . . .

The relationship between Frederic and Catherine often troubles cadets. Here, narrative distance offers students a means to forestall a young reader's hasty condemnation. Our talk of forestalling hasty condemnation needs some explanation. The goal is not to persuade cadets to adopt an ethic they may deplore. The goal is to get them to open up to the text, to hear the story, and to consider Frederic and Catherine as real human beings—people with character flaws, irrational impulses, good intentions, and the capacity to love. In what follows, we outline how we guide class discussions. . . .

Who is Frederic? A cad? A player? A guy in a war, acting like a guy in a war? Usually, students answer along such lines, and we encourage brief informal debate on the topic, but we always ask them to refrain from a final judgment until we have heard more of Frederic's story. But this passage offers more for critical readers to chew on. We help our students with a number of questions. Why does Frederic make this confession to his readers? More importantly, what does this confession do for the narrative? What difference would it make to the telling of the story had the narrator not told us that he lied to Catherine? We have our students read the passage, changing "I lied" to "I said." With that change, most readers get a feel for the delta separating the character Frederic from the narrator Frederic. The character Frederic has no reason to offer a confession. Only the narrator Frederic does. And in labeling the statement, he tells us something both of his vices and his virtues. Yes, he lied at the moment. But he recognizes the statement as a lie. We usually suggest to our students that the recognition of the character's lie is testimony to the narrator's veracity.

But Catherine is herself a character fraught with the complexities and contradictions revealed by a mask that simply won't stay in place. Is she duped by Frederic? She seems to be all too aware of the tacit motives and rules governing the interlude between herself and her would-be paramour:

> She looked down at the grass.
> "This is a rotten game we play, isn't it?"
> "What game?"
> "Don't be dull."
> "I'm not, on purpose."
> "You're a nice boy," she said. "And you play it as well as you know how. But it's a rotten game." (31)

We find class discussion of this passage helps young readers grasp the complexity of these characters and the narrator who tells their story. Throughout the novel, both characters make use of the word "crazy" to describe Catherine at times. How crazy is Catherine? What does the word mean in reference to her? There are a number of occasions when her behaviors or comments seem erratic or irrational. But the passage tells us that Catherine is not insane in any absolute sense of that word. Those times when she seems irrational may stem from having all too clear a comprehension of life's rotten games. Frederic the narrator reveals a woman who sees through all simulation. She knows Frederic's immediate motive and that his motive is only immediate. Yet, of her own volition, she embraces him in an intimate relationship.

The first step in the transformation of Frederic as cad to Frederic as lover comes after his injury on the battlefield. We have cadets examine the last half of chapter 14, where Frederic and Catherine are physically intimate for the first time. This passage, too, invites scrutiny in terms of narrative distance. We ask students to characterize the passage. For students in an introductory literature class, such a request can be quite challenging. Often they lack the vocabulary or reading experience to make an assessment of the passage. Again, we turn to their visual experience to get them started and ask, "If the book were made into a film, what MPAA rating would it get based on how this passage is presented?" This gets them thinking in terms of criteria with which they've become familiar through experience. As the discussion runs its course, we tell them that we characterize the feel of the passage as urgent but not graphic. That quality comes from what is conveyed without being specifically told. What does that tell us about the implied author? Can we distinguish between the implied author and the narrator here? The passion Frederic the character portrays suggests a person far too trapped in urgency to think in terms of good taste or virtue. But Frederic the narrator has had the advantage of time. Removed from the heat of the moment, he tells the story to admit to truth but not to descend into details of sordidness. What does that tell us of this narrator? Could this omission be a token of an enduring love? . . .

Strict discipline and compliance to regulations have always been a major component of overall instruction at the Air Force Academy, and the Hemingway code hero is a perfect literary role model for such behavior. Harkening back to the antiwar movement of the 1960s, and a questioning of the validity of military service itself, many English departments stopped teaching Hemingway altogether, largely because of a misperception of him as hawkish. The debate in the Air Force Academy's English department, however, unlike that in academia at large, wasn't about whether Hemingway should be taught, but which novel best demonstrated the virtues of the code hero, *The Sun Also Rises* or *A Farewell to Arms*. *Farewell* was selected, and it has been taught here for six decades.

The novel breathes life into what has become for too many cadets a threadbare phrase—the fog and friction of war. The novel compels students to grapple with war as a horror of human making, a thing that must be weighed against other things of human making, such as fear, courage, appetite, and love. As humans, we all are subject to failings and all are urged to pursue the higher virtues of our being. Both the failings and the virtues come at great price. With service comes the possibility of honor as well as the possibility of shame. With love comes the possibility of fulfillment as well as the possibility of ultimate loss. Moreover, one's end may be as much in the hands of fate as in the determination of the individual. We believe that if our cadets leave with a firm sense of the contingent in life, they are better prepared to serve their country.

Works by Ernest Hemingway

Three Stories and Ten Poems, 1923.

In Our Time, 1924.

In Our Time: Stories, 1925.

The Torrents of Spring, 1928.

Today Is Friday (pamphlet), 1926.

The Sun Also Rises, 1926.

Men Without Women, 1927.

A Farewell to Arms, 1929.

Death in the Afternoon, 1932.

God Rest You Merry Gentlemen (pamphlet), 1933.

Winner Take Nothing, 1933.

Green Hills of Africa, 1935.

To Have and Have Not, 1937.

The Spanish Earth (film transcript), 1938.

The Fifth Column and the First Forty-nine Stories, 1938.

For Whom the Bell Tolls, 1940.

Men at War: The Best War Stories of All Times (editor), 1942.

Voyage to Victory: An Eye-witness Report of the Battle for a Normandy Beachhead, 1944.

The Portable Hemingway, Ed., Malcolm Cowley, 1944.

Selected Short Stories, c. 1945.

The Essential Hemingway, 1947.

Across the River and into the Trees, 1950.

The Old Man and the Sea, 1952.

The Hemingway Reader, Ed., Charles Poore, 1953.

Two Christmas Tales, 1959.

Collected Poems, 1960.

The Snows of Kilimanjaro and Other Stories, 1961.

The Wild Years, Ed., Gene Z. Hanrahan, 1962.

A Moveable Feast, 1964.

By-Line: Ernest Hemingway: Selected Articles and Dispatches of Four Decades, Ed., William White, 1967.

The Fifth Column and Four Stories of the Spanish Civil War, 1969.

Ernest Hemingway, Cub Reporter, Ed., Matthew J. Bruccoli, 1970.

Islands in the Stream, 1970.

Ernest Hemingway's Apprenticeship: Oak Park 1916–1917, Ed., Matthew J. Bruccoli, 1971.

The Nick Adams Stories, 1972.

88 Poems, Ed., Nicholas Gerogiannis, 1979, 1992 (as *Complete Poems*).

Selected Letters 1917–1961, Ed., Carlos Baker, 1981.

The Dangerous Summer, 1985.

Dateline, Toronto: Hemingway's Complete "Toronto Star" Dispatches, 1920–1924, Ed., William White, 1985.

The Garden of Eden, 1986.

Complete Short Stories, 1987.

Remembering Spain: Hemingway's Civil War Eulogy and the Veterans of the Abraham Lincoln Brigade, Ed., Cary Nelson, 1994.

True at First Light, 1999.

Annotated Bibliography

Baker, Carlos. *Hemingway: The Writer as Artist*. Princeton: Princeton University Press, 1972, fourth edition (first edition 1952).

This volume is essential reading for devoted students of Hemingway's life and work, not only because the author is among the most prominent of Hemingway scholars, but because the work includes important revisions of material that was incomplete and/or incorrect when supplied for the first, second, and third editions. For example, Baker includes chapters on two posthumously published works—*A Moveable Feast* (1964) and *Islands in the Stream* (1970). Baker's scholarship brings together important insights about Hemingway, the man and the writer, and his published works.

Boker, Pamela A. *The Grief Taboo in American Literature: Loss and Prolonged Adolescence in Twain, Melville, and Hemingway*. New York and London: New York University Press, 1996.

This study of American literature brings together the insights from two disciplines—Freudian psychoanalysis and literary criticism. The author, trained in both fields, moves away from the earlier notion of the American male as a self-orphaned and self-reliant hero to a view of American male figures posing as heroes to conceal from themselves and others feelings of deprivation and loss. Recent insights about feminine sensibilities, proposed and promoted by feminist literary critics, are brought to bear on many of the classic American novels centering on male protagonists.

Donaldson, Scott. *By Force of Will: The Life and Art of Ernest Hemingway*. New York: Viking Press, 1977.

Donaldson is widely considered among the most prominent critics and scholars of Hemingway and this book, in particular, is accessible to students at all levels of inquiry. The chapters are focused on themes of particular relevance for the writer; "Sport," "Politics," "Art," "Death," "Religion," and "Sex" are examples.

119

———, ed. *New Essays on "A Farewell to Arms."* Cambridge: Cambridge University Press, 1990.

This volume of critical commentary introduces the reader to many of the essential themes and issues traditionally associated with Hemingway's second novel. The editor, a prominent Hemingway scholar, offers a wealth of background information about the writing and publishing of the novel, including details about the censorship problems it generated. Other issues discussed include a retrospective look at the changing critical reception to the character of Catherine; some speculation about why Hemingway chose to write about the aftermath of the war (*The Sun Also Rises*, 1926) before writing about the war itself (*A Farewell to Arms*, 1929); and an analysis of some particularities of Hemingway's stylistic and language choices.

Fantina, Richard. *Ernest Hemingway: Machismo and Masochism.* New York: Palgrave Macmillan, 2005.

This study of Hemingway focuses on one aspect of the man and his writings—his longtime association with the traditionally male attribute of machismo and its connection to the concept of masochism. Hemingway has been praised and criticized for his fictional representation of the stereotypical "all-American" male who pursues dangerous challenges in the natural world more vigorously than he pursues women. The Hemingway male character is attracted to and loves women, but, for varying reasons, appears incapable of sustaining strong heterosexual relationships. Most feminist critics, in particular, have found Hemingway not to their liking. The posthumous publication of *The Garden of Eden* in 1986 initiated a serious re-examination of this view of Hemingway. Fantina is writing from within this more recent assessment with the purpose of demonstrating a substantial masochistic element in Hemingway's most famous male heroes and a related attribution of conventional male characteristics to his "ideal" women in *The Sun Also Rises* (1926), *A Farewell to Arms* (1929), and *Across the River and into the Trees* (1950).

Gandal, Keith. *The Gun and the Pen: Hemingway, Fitzgerald, Faulkner, and the Fiction of Mobilization.* New York: Oxford University Press, 2008.

Drawing on archival documents from World War I, the author argues that an important shift in military needs led to a little-discussed change in attitude toward American masculinity that influenced the three major writers of the postwar decade—Hemingway, Fitzgerald, and Faulkner. Gandal contends that the military's need for the language skills of certain ethnic American groups, such as Italian Americans, made it more likely that promotion in the ranks would fall to members of those groups, leaving "all-American" male soldiers at a disadvantage. Gandal notes that none of the three writers served in traditional military roles and none was directly engaged in combat, and this "failing" influenced the way each wrote about the war and its victims. In his discussion of *Farewell*, Gandal points to the tension between Lieutenant Moretti and Frederic Henry.

Oldsey, Bernard. *Hemingway's Hidden Craft: The Writing of "A Farewell to Arms."* University Park and London: The Pennsylvania State University Press, 1979.

This study of the way Hemingway's *A Farewell to Arms* was conceived, developed, and published was prompted by its half-century of critical and popular success. Oldsey examines the multiple manuscripts of the novel that Hemingway was working on at different times and makes well-informed surmises about why the author made the final choices that he did. Among the interesting details in the book are the multiple titles Hemingway considered and the 39 revisions of the ending he found necessary to make.

Oliver, Charles M., ed. *Ernest Hemingway's "A Farewell to Arms": A Documentary Volume.* Farmington, MI: Thomas Gale, 2005.

This extensive reference book for *A Farewell to Arms* is volume 308 in the Dictionary of Literary Biography series, generally located in college libraries. It is a source of information on every aspect of the novel including the earliest author drafts; editing, publishing, and reprinting details; historical and cultural background materials; early, middle, and recent critical reception; controversies; and lists of works by and about Hemingway and *A Farewell to Arms*.

Sanderson, Rena, ed. *Hemingway's Italy: New Perspectives*. Baton Rouge: Louisiana State University Press, 2006.

After his first trip to Italy—with many more to follow— Hemingway wrote to Captain James Gamble, his supervisor in the war and good friend: "I'm so homesick for Italy that when I write about it it has that something about it that you only get in a love letter" (2). According to the editor of this collection of essays on Hemingway's connection to Italy, the young American writer found Italy to be a version of paradise—especially in contrast to the morally righteous ambiance of Oak Park—and, upon return, a paradise lost. The essays deal with various aspects of his time spent there and lessons learned. His Italian experiences made their appearance in several of his novels, most prominently in *A Farewell to Arms* (1929) but also in *Death in the Afternoon* (1932), "The Snows of Kilimanjaro" (1936), "A Natural History of the Dead" (1928), and *In Our Time: Stories* (1925).

Strychacz, Thomas. *Hemingway's Theaters of Masculinity*. Baton Rouge: Louisiana State University Press, 2003.

This work on Hemingway is among several recent studies that challenge long-established views of the writer's aims and attitudes, specifically, as the title suggests, the writer's representation of masculinity. Using insights associated with deconstruction theories, Strychacz argues that Hemingway's notions about masculinity and the process of "becoming a man" depend on their theatrical context and the particular audience they are intended for. Although *Farewell* is not one of the major novels considered in this study, Strychacz writes interestingly about the different types of posturing Frederic Henry assumes as a war hero.

Tyler, Lisa, ed. *Teaching Hemingway's* A Farewell to Arms. Kent, Ohio: Kent State University Press, 2008.

The essays in this book have been collected by and for teachers in high schools and colleges, but they offer insights about the novel of interest to any reader. The contributors write from diverse perspectives and for diverse objectives making this an especially valuable companion for studying Hemingway. For example, two retired professors who taught at the United States Air Force Academy discuss the differences in background between cadets heading for a military career and students at traditional schools, and how these differences affected the cadets' reaction to the grim depiction of war in *A Farewell to Arms*. Another essay clarifies which details in the novel are genuinely autobiographical and which are the product of Hemingway's extensive research.

Vernon, Alex. *Soldiers Once and Still: Ernest Hemingway, James Salter, and Tim O'Brien*. Iowa City: University of Iowa Press, 2004.

In his preface, Alex Vernon notes that between the generation that fought in (or resisted) the Vietnam War (the generation of leaders currently in power) and now (2003, the time of his writing—the beginning of the U.S. involvement in the war in Iraq), most living Americans have had no immediate or personal sense of the realities of wartime life and combat. Keeping in mind his own combat experience and the increasing likelihood that the youth of this generation will undergo some firsthand experience of warfare, Vernon's concern is to bring more public attention to the existing narrative representations of the "human dimension of war in order to understand war better when it beckons" (ix). He divides the volume into three sections, each devoted to the work and influence of a writer who is also a veteran.

 # Contributors

Harold Bloom is Sterling Professor of the Humanities at Yale University. He is the author of 30 books, including *Shelley's Mythmaking*, *The Visionary Company*, *Blake's Apocalypse*, *Yeats*, *A Map of Misreading*, *Kabbalah and Criticism*, *Agon: Toward a Theory of Revisionism*, *The American Religion*, *The Western Canon*, and *Omens of Millennium: The Gnosis of Angels, Dreams, and Resurrection*. *The Anxiety of Influence* sets forth Professor Bloom's provocative theory of the literary relationships between the great writers and their predecessors. His most recent books include *Shakespeare: The Invention of the Human*, a 1998 National Book Award finalist, *How to Read and Why*, *Genius: A Mosaic of One Hundred Exemplary Creative Minds*, *Hamlet: Poem Unlimited*, *Where Shall Wisdom Be Found?*, and *Jesus and Yahweh: The Names Divine*. In 1999, Professor Bloom received the prestigious American Academy of Arts and Letters Gold Medal for Criticism. He has also received the International Prize of Catalonia, the Alfonso Reyes Prize of Mexico, and the Hans Christian Andersen Bicentennial Prize of Denmark.

Carlos Baker, Hemingway's main biographer, was Woodrow Wilson Professor of Literature at Princeton University. Among his scholarly publications are *Shelley's Major Poetry* and *Ernest Hemingway: A Life Story*.

Pamela A. Boker is the author of *Death in American Literature: Critical Essays* (1996).

Thomas Strychacz teaches English at Mills College in California. Among his published works are *Modernism, Mass Culture, and Professionalism* (1993) and *Dangerous Masculinities* (2008). His scholarly interests include American literature, mass culture, and popular and cultural approaches to literature.

124

Alex Vernon attended West Point Military Academy and served in a combat unit during the (first) Persian Gulf War (1990–91). He is assistant professor of English at Hendrix College.

Richard Fantina participated in the Hemingway International Conference in Key West, Florida, in 2004. He teaches English at the University of Miami. He was the editor of the *Journal of Latin American Anthropology* and of the book *Straight Writ Queer: Non-Normative Expressions of Heterosexuality in Literature* (2006).

John Robert Bittner, before his death in 2002, taught at the School of Journalism and Mass Communication at the University of North Carolina at Chapel Hill. His scholarly interests included Hemingway and his writings.

Robert E. Fleming, Professor Emeritus of English at the University of New Mexico, wrote *The Face in the Mirror: Hemingway's Writers* (1994), edited *Hemingway and the Natural World* (1999), and contributed articles on Hemingway's life and work to *American Literature*, the *Hemingway Review*, *Journal of Modern Literature*, and the *North Dakota Quarterly*, among other journals. With Robert W. Lewis, Fleming co-edited Hemingway's posthumously published African book, *Under Kilimanjaro* (2005).

Ellen Andrews Knodt teaches English at Pennsylvania State University. She has written for the *Hemingway Review* and the *North Dakota Quarterly* and contributed essays to *Teaching Hemingway's "The Sun Also Rises"* (Peter L. Hayes, ed.) and *Teaching Hemingway's "A Farewell to Arms."* She recently won the Atherton Award for Excellence in Teaching.

Keith Gandal teaches English at Northern Illinois State University. He is the author of *The Virtues of the Vicious: Jacob Riis, Stephen Crane, and the Spectacle of the Slum* (1997).

James H. Meredith is a retired professor of English at the United States Air Force Academy. He is currently serving as president of the Ernest Hemingway Foundation and Society. His most recently published works are *Understanding the Literature of World War II* (1999) and *Understanding the Literature of World War I* (2004).

Jackson A. Niday II is a retired professor of English at the United States Air Force Academy. His areas of specialization are rhetorical theory and war literature. He is an associate editor of *War, Literature, and the Arts.*

Acknowledgments

Carlos Baker, "The Mountain and the Plain." From *Hemingway: The Writer as Artist*, pp. 98–101. © 1952 Princeton University Press, 1956 2nd. Edition, 1980 renewed in author's name. Reprinted by permission of Princeton University Press.

Pamela A. Boker, "The Shaping of Hemingway's Art of Repressed Grief: Mother-Loss and Father-Hunger from *In Our Time* to *Winner Take Nothing*." From *The Grief Taboo in American Literature: Loss and Prolonged Adolescence in Twain, Melville, and Hemingway*, pp. 197–201, 332. © 1996 by New York University.

Thomas Strychacz, "Hemingway's Theaters of War: *A Farewell to Arms* and *For Whom the Bell Tolls*." From Hemingway's *Theaters of Masculinity*, pp. 87–91. © 2003 by Louisiana State University Press.

Alex Vernon, "War, Gender, and Ernest Hemingway." Reprinted from *Soldiers Once and Still*, pp. 77–81, 278. © 2004 by the University of Iowa Press.

Richard Fantina, "Defying the Code: Masochism in the Major Texts." From *Ernest Hemingway: Machismo and Masochism*, pp. 115–16, 180. © Richard Fontina, 2005. Published by and reproduced with permission of Palgrave Macmillan.

John Robert Bittner, "Anti-Fascist Symbols and Subtexts in *A Farewell to Arms*: Hemingway, Mussolini, and Journalism in the 1920s." From *Hemingway's Italy: New Perspectives*, Rena Sanderson, ed., pp. 103–07. © 2006 by Louisiana State University Press.

Robert E. Fleming, "Ettore Moretti: Hemingway's 'Legitimate War Hero?'" From *Hemingway's Italy: New Perspectives*, Rena

128

Index